Second Choice
growing up adopted

Second Choice
growing up adopted

Robert Andersen, M.D.

1993
Badger Hill Press
Chesterfield, Missouri

First printed 1993

10 9 8 7 6 5 4 3 2 1

Manufactured in the United States of America.

Library of Congress Catalog Number: 92-90502

International Standard Book Number: 0-9632648-4-2

Badger Hill Press
Post Office Box 4066
Chesterfield, Missouri 63006-4066

For Paul and Erika, in lieu of a legacy.

Acknowledgements:

I would like to thank my friends for their encouragement, criticism, and suggestions; they have significantly contributed to the evolution of this book. Special thanks goes to Joanne Fehling, who assiduously worked to eliminate the "brain dead" portions of the manuscript. Special thanks also goes to Suzanne Byrne, of Byron Byrne & Associates, for her editorial and technical assistance. Writing this book has been a satisfying experience, in part, because of the people who worked with me. Finishing the book leaves a temporary, but definite, void.

When the sun is shining, one does not ask for the moon.

—*Russian proverb*

Contents

This is me. I'm not very old.

Introduction

This book deals with adoption—specifically, infant adoption. It also deals with me—an adoptee and a psychiatrist. I began the book as an attempt to organize my thinking about growing up adopted. Ten years ago, following a lifetime of suppression, I finally realized that my adoption played a major role in my development. But the issues remained unclear. Adoption issues are abstract and diffuse and often play themselves out in areas seemingly far removed from adoption. I hoped writing would help identify and clarify these issues. I believe it has.

The book originates from two perspectives. The first part (chapters one through ten) describes my life and derives largely from my perspective as an adoptee. The latter part (chapters eleven through thirteen) analyzes the consequences of my adoption and arises more from my perspective as a psychiatrist.

My childhood history consists of two stories. One story is open, fully conscious, superficial, relatively cheerful, and excludes adoption. This part contains fireflies, circuses, and walks to the soda fountain. The other is sad, secret, problematic, shameful, and includes adoption. The second part involves promiscuity, abandonment, black markets, illegitimacy, and illegality. In this book I intend to look back with my current information and attempt to integrate these two disparate stories.

My major thesis contends that adoption is inherently traumatic, that an adoptive family differs from a natural one, and that this trauma and these differences are better managed if they are recognized rather than repressed. The public tends to glorify adoption, "in mass empathy with childless couples, seeing it as a lucky break (rescue) for the infants." This book does not endorse that tendency. Psychological consequences follow from being adopted. Society does not obviate these consequences by glorifying the situation.

As a point of style, I chose to use the masculine pronoun in situations not gender specific. This was easier than keeping everything neutral, and I chose masculine because it fits better with my personal history. Actually, women do most of the writing, searching, and reflecting on adoption issues. That this book was written by a male makes it relatively unique.

Honesty guided the writing of this book. This fact will not solidify some of my past relationships, but neither will it generate any mortal enemies. Dishonesty guided the management of my adoption. I found it therapeutic to reverse the process.

Chapter One
Childhood

Twas my one Glory—
Let it be
Remembered
I was owned of Thee—
—Emily Dickinson

Little about Milwaukee in mid-March recommends it. Winter remains, but without its splendor, and early hints of spring merely serve to soften one's resolve to tolerate the bitter cold. In March 1940, somewhere in a two-story, wood frame house in a Milwaukee residential neighborhood, my mother awaited my birth. I have never seen my mother and was told she has never seen me. I know for sure about this woman only that she did not keep me and that she left me in a home that sold babies through the black market. I prefer to think she did not personally profit from my transaction.

In Racine, twenty-five miles south of Milwaukee, the Andersens also awaited my birth. Stanley and Ann Andersen wanted a child, although like most adoptive parents they preferred a girl. Because I was born a boy, they almost canceled the arrangement with the maternity home. I assume that my birthmother came to this home for reasons common to unwed mothers. Stanley and Ann Andersen came there because they could not obtain a child any other way. The two parties never met. They never will.

Residents of Wisconsin who could not have their own children did not rush to my maternity home to buy a child. People chose this place last, not first. The Andersens' first chose to adopt a foster child, Joanne, whom they had taken in for two years following Ann's hysterectomy. But Joanne's mother would not allow this. In fact, she insisted the girl be moved to a different family. The Andersens then went to adoption agencies, but for reasons that remain unclear, the state deemed them unsuitable as adoptive parents.

Following this development Ann became depressed. She began to think about suicide. At this point the Andersens heard about and acted on the black-market option. A few years ago Stanley confessed this fact to me. Ashamed that they had obtained me through the black market, he thought I would hate him for revealing this truth. He was wrong; I did not hate him for the truth—the lies bothered me more, and while hate is too strong a word, it leads in the right direction.

I grew up thinking the Andersens were my natural parents. Actually, they were not even my adoptive parents. My birthparents retained legal custody until I was fourteen, although they could not have known this. The Andersens raised me. I thought of them as my parents. But I am now convinced that we read from different pages in our relationship because of our disparity of knowledge about my position in the family.

Conscious concerns about adoption, dual parents, and black markets did not therefore fill my childhood. Puppy dogs, toboggans, and garter snakes comprised the business of the day. While those things stand out most readily from my childhood, the adoption issues did not become inconsequential. My adoption issues remained less conscious than puppy dogs and garter snakes, but became more important. Puppy dogs and garter snakes are tangible; they are obvious, visible, and one does not need to infer their existence. Adoption issues are abstract, intangible, and difficult to identify. In my case, they also remained secret, which made them even harder to recognize. I now believe that my position in the Andersen family influenced my development more than any other environmental factor.

We lived in Racine, an attractive city on the shore of Lake Michigan, until I was eight. My mother often boasted that the city headquartered seven nationally known corporations, the most famous being Johnson's Wax. My father worked for one of these national corporations, the Oster Company, known in the 1940s for hair clippers and electric motors, but now known more for Osterizers. Racine, like much of the midwest machine belt, has not prospered over the past thirty years. It no longer houses seven national corporations and its downtown sits partially deserted. While major improvements have recently been added to the harbor, the city may never recapture its former stature.

I have many pleasant memories of Racine. We lived in a small but adequate house that looks as well kept today as it did forty years ago. Downtown Racine ran along the lake front. Uptown Racine lay somewhere north, a long way from where we lived, but on the way to my favorite aunt and uncle's apartment. I do not know if people still use the terms downtown and uptown today, especially since the advent of shopping centers.

Downtown, on the beach, the circus would pitch its tents in the summertime. Downtown also sported sailboats, elevators, and movie theaters, as well as a giant model of the harbor at the government center, and two long piers on the lake from which one could catch glimpses of perch and other fish. I often made the six-mile trip downtown with my mother. Racine is quite cold in the winter, but my childhood memories run more to sleds, toboggans, and snowmen than to slush, shoveling, and dead batteries.

I spent much more time with my mother than with my father. She and I went on walks to the soda fountain, took bus rides downtown, and played games in our backyard. Mother managed the house, so she was usually available to provide assistance if something went wrong with my latest adventure. Father and I did little together, although at times I would accompany him to the Danish Brotherhood. The Danish Brotherhood ran slot machines, and I once won a jackpot on the penny machine—three hundred or more coins—at a time when pennies were used for more than collecting dust in jars on a shelf. The machines were illegal, which made playing them all the more fun. My father liked to take me to the Brotherhood because I could beat some of his peers at cribbage. The Andersens and several other couples heard about the black-market maternity home through the Danish Brotherhood. I always enjoyed going there and am sure they did more at the Brotherhood than play slots and broker babies.

My family often went fishing, usually with Frank and Lois, my favorite uncle and aunt. Those were the glory days for fishing in Wisconsin, as they were for Racine as well. In the 1940s the lampreys had yet to kill the lake trout, the beaches remained open, and the city's downtown had not capitulated to the malls. We caught buckets of fish off the piers in Racine harbor. The Andersens viewed fishing as central to their idea of recreation. Somehow I lost interest in the sport. Maybe it's genetic.

To this day I idealize Racine. We moved to Palo Alto, California, when I was seven, and by all standards Palo Alto, the home of Stanford University, has much more going for it than rust-belt Racine. Yet for me Racine has magic unlike anywhere else, even though I have lived in some of America's garden spots. In recent years, when my search led me to believe I had been born in Tennessee, the magic shifted to Memphis and

Racine lost its fascination. My feeling for these cities resembles a romance, albeit a fickle one. Today I am in love again with Wisconsin. I guess if people have a close feeling of family and grow up in the Northwest Territories they will be conditioned to love even permafrost and five-month nights.

With Mother (on my right) and Aunt Lois.

Ten years ago if I had been writing a history of my childhood, I would simply have continued with the above line of stuff—fishing trips, moving to California, Little League baseball—maybe throwing in my favorite foods, colors, and movies. I cannot do that today. My childhood did not merely consist of uptowns, downtowns, snips, snails, and puppy dog tails. I was, after all, a bastard, from questionable stock, abandoned by my natural parents, sold through the black market, and disconnected biologically, as well as legally, from every human being in my world. The adoption issues did not fade away like the April snow, and while I did not understand them as such, they persisted and significantly determined who I became.

My childhood adoption issues prove more difficult to consider today than such things as city geography and how well

I played marbles. Not knowing about my adoption, I do not re-member adoption issues as such. So while I can recall that my best friend, Jimmy Hansen, lived across the street and his father drove a Buick, I do not remember, for example, such things as my adoptive mother telling me my natural mother was a nurse (or a trollop), my adoptive father confessing he would have pre-ferred to adopt a girl, or myself fretting as to why my natural mother gave me away. I cannot reach back and recall an adop-tion issue the same way I might recall that we had a coal bin in the basement. Still, it seems plausible that with my current knowledge of the situation, some understanding of psychology, and a few reasonable assumptions, I can today identify feelings and memories that are most likely adoption related. I hope to do so, for this book is an attempt to understand the psychological consequences of growing up biologically disconnected; and such issues do not always identify themselves with a red flag and the letter "A." My ignorance about the adoption changed at age twelve, when I learned I was not the Andersens' natural child. But this revelation did not make the adoption issues self-evident, for a lack of information is not the only thing that can impede understanding.

Being uninformed about my adoption did not prevent me from perceiving its effects—one can more easily hide the cogni-tive than the emotional component of behavior, just as one can more easily conceal the content of a secret than conceal the sec-ret itself. While as a child I did not know specifically that my parents were worried I might be removed from their home, I was able to perceive that something about our relationship troubled them. Similarly, I did not know my mother was depressed because she could not have her own children, and would not have understood what it meant to be depressed, but I could perceive that she was not happy. I did not know my parents kept secrets from me, but my experience indicated we were not close. Being spared the details was not a blessing, for when a child knows something is wrong but does not know why, he blames himself for the difficulties.

Stanley and Ann Andersen did not feel that buying and raising a black-market baby fit in well with their usual activities. To the degree that they felt a need for secrecy, they must have also appreciated a problem; and I could not escape being a central player in this "problem." Maybe it worked well for them to ignore the adoption, but it has not worked for me. One does not build a house on a sandbar or a personality on a pile of problematic secrets. Feeling secure about oneself is difficult when basic aspects are unknown and frightening. It is all too easy to worry about what might be at the core of the secrets, with the possibilities limited only by one's imagination. Fur and fangs? A career of stealing horses? Brigandage? Might I find myself some night inexplicably sharpening an ax or two? (Two-thirds of America's great mass murderers have been adoptees.) Should I warn you that you might be reading this book at your own risk? Today I realize it is getting late for me to turn into a second Son of Sam, but as a teenager I did not find the movie *The Bad Seed* (she kills people because of her genetic makeup) entertaining. Maybe the time has come to face the dragons. After all, I do not personally have anything against dragons.

I look like a bootlegger. I wouldn't
let my children play with this kid.

Chapter Two

More childhood

No themes are so human as those that reflect for us, out of the confusion of life, the close connection of bliss and bale, of the things that help with the things that hurt, so dangling before us forever that bright hard medal, of so strange an alloy, one face of which is somebody's right and ease and the other somebody's pain and wrong.

—*Henry James*

I need to review my dark-side history to get a full picture of my childhood. As stated earlier, the Andersens preferred to adopt a girl. When my mother delivered a boy, they were inclined to wait for another child. The home had to struggle to convince them just to come up and look at me. The Andersens were told that my father was a doctor and my mother a nurse. This doctor-nurse story ranks number two in adoption lies, right behind the one about the birthparents being killed in an automobile accident. (Adoption organizations could double as support groups for people having lost parents in auto accidents.) I do not know if the information about my birthparents was correct, but the Andersens believed it to be so. Apparently the children from this home came without papers, which depresses me because I would feel more like a thoroughbred with official papers. Several years ago Stanley said there was no original birth certificate. I cannot trust the information given to me by my adoptive parents, since they generally lied about the adoption, but in later years my father became somewhat more honest. Also, independent reason suggests there was no original birth certificate: I have located two other adoptees who came through this black-market home and neither has an original. In one case, the parents paid a physician to falsify the birth certificate, listing themselves as the natural parents. In the other case, handled much like mine, the family did not adopt the girl until she turned fifteen, at which time they obtained a delayed certificate of birth without there being an original. Karl Sorenson, one of the customers, said, "Getting a child from this maternity home was like picking up a sack of potatoes."

I must have impressed the Andersens enough for them to take me home. Certainly it was nothing I did—perhaps having twenty digits, ten on each side, did not hurt. My adoptive father said he never met my mother, although at the time only one or two walls separated them. Being a residential house, the children were shown in the living room, while the mothers remained out of sight somewhere to the rear. The manager told my parents it would be easier on my birthmother if they took me on the spot, because she hadn't yet seen me and not doing so would somehow benefit her.

I do not know the specifics of the transaction, but can surmise the Andersens came prepared to take me home. While only twenty-five miles separates Racine from Milwaukee, Stanley and Ann did not have a car and had to arrange a ride with a neighbor. Thus they most likely came prepared to make the deal, provided I did not have gill slits or fur. They paid $250, probably in cash—equivalent to about $4,000 today, not a trivial amount.   But I have an adoptee friend whose parents paid $20,000 for her, and you can imagine how it feels to compare her selling price to my unimpressive $250—I have to remind myself that the Baltimore Colts got Johnny Unitas for $50.

Me again. Age five or six.

The situation calmed down for the Andersens when they finally got a child and took him (me) home. A few months later the maternity home offered them another child, this time a girl.

The Andersens declined, probably because they could not afford another child. Later still, the home solicited a "donation," ostensibly to help the residents. My father viewed the request as blackmail. He exchanged some unpleasantries with the manager and ended their relationship.

The factory-outlet nature of my placement precluded any warm, fuzzy (and usually mindless) tales from attaching to the story of my adoption. Most adoptees are subject to a number of such anecdotes, which pop up around adoption like toadstools in a compost heap. The most common fable is the adoptee as "chosen child," which points out that natural parents have to accept the children they produce whereas adoptive parents get to choose. This factor is supposed to make the adoptee feel good about himself. I have never appreciated the chosen-child story, mainly because it is untrue. In addition, it conjures up images of adoptive parents strolling through three-and-a-half-acre baby showrooms, picking the cream of the crop from a supply of hundreds. People never had much choice, even in the 1940s, and today the demand for babies certainly outweighs the supply. Besides the mere untruth of it, other aspects discredit this tale. For one, it brings to mind too easily the analogy of a trip to the city dog pound. While I would rather be compared to a puppy than a patio set, neither flatters especially well. Also, the story defies logic, which should be obvious to anyone who retains consciousness. The problem, of course, is that to be chosen you must first be rejected. The term *chosen* evokes the word *special* in the phrase "Special School District," where *special* really means "not suitable for regular school."

Nevertheless, adoptees frequently claim that being chosen made them special: "Others were expected, I was selected." If this fable works for them, great. Luckily the story did not appeal to me because in my case it clearly did not apply. Several years ago my father told me some details of my placement, stressing how much he and Ann wanted a girl. Cognitive difficulties impaired his judgement at the time he told me these things, and while his remote memory remained relatively intact, he could not readily appreciate the implications of his statements. Fortunately I did not embrace the chosen-child story, for Stanley thoroughly discredited it. I was vaguely amused by his open preference for a girl, and he certainly attested to his veracity, since his story would have made a ridiculous lie.

Ann Andersen had big problems in her life at the time of my placement. Only twenty-five years old, she had undergone a hysterectomy and radiation treatment for uterine cancer. This did not build confidence, and a question remained about her chances for a five-year survival. She would never have her own children, would have no more menstrual periods, and became low on estrogens at a time when sex and hormones was a

Mom and me in Chicago, May 1946.

hot topic and Premarin remained twenty-five years away. Ann had lost a foster child who had been with her for two years. Finally, the state certified her unsuitable as an adoptive parent, and she could obtain a child only by breaking the law and wiping out the family savings.

Depressed and thinking about suicide, she viewed me as a solution to her problems. But bringing me home did not cure her depression. I came and her depression continued, although she probably appreciated having me there. Her depression never incapacitated her, and following my arrival she apparently did not again consider suicide. Perhaps I served usefully in that respect.

My memories of Mother's depression are emotional rather than cognitive. I cannot recall, for example, Father telling me that Mom is depressed and what the world needs is a good tri-cyclic antidepressant. I can recall endless hours together with nothing happening. Mother used to stare out the window for long periods at a time. Yet, she did her housework well and took good physical care of me. More than that, I think she loved me. Her attachment created a problem for her because the more she loved me the more vulnerable she became to a stranger arriving at her door wanting to take me back.

Using me as an antidepressant did not work because Ann's depression and my adoption were essentially separate issues. If her depression had been due to a lack of opportunity to parent, then having me around might have been helpful. But my presence could not affect the issues of health, infertility, sexuality, marital conflict, and so on. The Andersens brought me into their family to improve Ann Andersen's mood. To the degree she remained depressed, I could be seen as failing; and Stanley and Ann expected more in this regard than they received. Also, I was not a girl. This fact became irrelevant to my mother, but not to my father, who could often be seen at the Andersen family gatherings sitting with a little girl on his lap, but never with a little boy. (I have two children myself, and Stanley's blatant preference for my daughter offended my son.)

No one told me I was doing a poor job with my mother's depression or that I should have been a girl, but these issues existed in my life and people react to the totality of their situation, rather than just to the paid political announcements. Somewhere in the early experience of what I have learned to call myself is the diffuse, implicit reflection of the Andersens' disap-pointment and their judgment that finds me wanting.

Thank heaven for school. Something was always going on at school and I usually did well at it. Falling short at home, I could score some points at school; I was lucky that way. When we played dodgeball, I often remained the last in the circle. (That was good.) When we played softball, I often hit the ball the farthest. I won the spelling contests, drew the best animals, obtained good grades, and got along well with everyone. When we chose teams, I usually did the choosing. My birthmother may have put me up for sale, but she left me with some abilities that proved a godsend in the difficult times.

I do not want to give the impression that my childhood divided into unpleasant things at home and pleasant things away. Some pleasant things happened at home. The Andersens and I shared a life, and we conducted the business of life together. They were nice-enough people. The business of our lives ran smoothly. We were not rich, but also not poor. My parents had no major vices, and their marriage remained stable. Bound together in time and space, if not in spirit, we shared good and bad times. Necessity joined us together in problematic circumstances, and we made the best of it; but we probably would not have chosen each other had the circumstances been different.

In the visible world I passed as normal. I played in a band, made the Little League all-star team, and earned ten Boy Scout merit badges en route to becoming a star-level scout and being elected senior patrol leader. I was well liked at school, worked from age ten, saved most of my money, and stayed out of trouble. My grades were good. My chores got done. I loved animals. And I was healthy. All that for $250!

Counting base hits or merit badges, one would have concluded I was getting along fine, but on the inside things fared less well. Although the Andersens could not fault my actions, they criticized my feelings—I could never meet their expectations for emotional responsiveness. How well I did in school or sports mattered less to Stanley and Ann than how I felt about them being my parents. They always wanted more appreciation, enthusiasm, and testimony for and about the quality of their parenting than I was able to provide. Not really parents, neither biological nor adoptive, the Andersens probably felt insecure as parents. They expected me regularly to assure them all was well, but I could not comply to the degree they required. Their expectations were impossible to meet, but I did not see that at the time. In retrospect, it appears the Andersens approached me with ambivalence and expected conviction, lied and expected trust, drew boundaries and expected unity. Had I understood things in that way, I could have reacted differently. But as a child I did not see my parents' limitations and merely faulted myself for not meeting their expectations. My external successes failed to neutralize the shortcomings I attributed to myself as a person, and I progressively became a more troubled individual. Being uninformed about my position in the family did not in any way foster my development.

Almost any situation at home could generate emotional conflicts. Christmases provide an example. Every Christmas I received presents accompanied by the admonition that because of the gifts I should be more considerate of my parents, usually for the entire ensuing year. This annual holiday message presented two problems: First, the message implied that I must by nature be inconsiderate. Second, since I never entirely liked my gifts, I also had to worry about being unappreciative. My best-ever Christmas present was a puppy, but he came from my grandparents. My parents rarely got the things I really wanted —a basketball they gave me at age twelve illustrates this point. My two best friends and I were all destined to one day play college basketball. We played well, even at age twelve, and could readily tell the difference between good and bad equipment. My Christmas basketball might have worked fine at the beach, but not on the court. I simply never used it. Was this inappropriate equipment, or did I expect to much? I could never tell. Birthdays resembled Christmases in this respect. To this day, presents cause me problems because I worry about appearing unappreciative.

I did not write this book to complain about my childhood presents. I do not intend, nor think it would be useful, to compare whether adoptees are treated better or worse than nonadoptees. Also, it matters little to me personally whether state legislatures open or close adoption records; unless they pass laws forcing adoptees to use inferior basketballs, I will not notice what the legislatures do. What matters to me are the differences between adoptive and natural families and the consequences of these differences on the family members. More specifically, I care about what happens when these differences are unrecognized, ignored, or suppressed. The suppression caused me my biggest problems as an adoptee.

Getting the wrong basketball was a disappointment. Not having a birth certificate, being given away by my birthmother, growing up with people who would rather not have met me, and being sold were other disappointments. But while unfortunate, these things were not personal indictments—i.e., not essentially of my doing. Disappointments of this type reside outside the person. One adjusts to them, gets over them. External disappointments remain outside a person's identity. Life consists of a series of losses, which by themselves do not cause psychopathology. How a person reacts to a loss largely determines whether there will be subsequent emotional problems, not the loss itself. One does better to confront a loss directly; ignoring it or wrapping it with platitudes may obviate the need for grief over the short term, but invites a problem with self-esteem over the long term.

If people recognize the adoption as important, they can use it to explain experience—problems can be understood in the context of the adoption. For example, an adoption-related explanation of the basketball issue might assume that because the Andersens lacked athletic experience themselves, they encountered difficulty empathizing with my athletic needs. The problem could be conceptualized as having involved differences in biologically determined abilities and interests between the Andersens and myself; it resided in the adoption situation itself (i.e., no one was at fault). An explanation excluding the adoption cannot envision problems as being situational and therefore usually has to explain problems on the basis of personalities. Such an explanation might find the Andersens to have been inattentive or myself ungrateful. Usually with this type of explanation people point their fingers at the adoptee, frequently with some reference to genetic limitations. When this happens often enough, the adoptee absorbs it.

I saw myself as different from my parents, accurately so, although we differed more in aptitudes and interests than in physical appearance. Physically, I passed as an Andersen. My father stood slightly less than six-feet tall, my mother reached a little more than five-feet tall, and I grew to six-foot-one. Ann's parents came from Czechoslovakia, Stanley's came from Denmark, and my grandparents, perhaps, from Germany. We all had brown hair and relatively light complexions. My father's eyes were blue, as are mine. People said I looked like my father, but they were just being polite. Still, anyone seeing our family would not be forced to think adoption.

The Andersens participated in activities requiring less physical activity than I could endure, and they expected me (not insistently) to conform to their ways. My activities normally involved playing catch, dribbling a basketball, or riding my bike, whereas Mother spent her time doing crossword puzzles or looking out the window, and Father enjoyed talking on his amateur radio. I never talked on his radio and have yet to do a crossword puzzle. Not feeling like a member of the family and not experiencing relationships in the prescribed manner, I began to view myself as deficient. Unaware of the adoption issues, I created my own explanation for my shortcomings and concluded that my faults came from being an only child. It appeared that having brothers and sisters, as did my parents, made one a better person. Siblings made one sensitive, understanding, empathic, and good. Siblings made one a better human being, and I was, alas, an only child. My status as an only child would never change.

I developed two views of myself. One view, based on the kind of person I felt myself to be, looked bad. The other, based on what I could do, looked better. An outsider would probably not have noticed this conflict, for people fail to see such things clearly in children. After all, even an eventual serial killer or a United States President (actual adoptee examples) will not distinguish himself as such at age seven or eight. With time, however, my problems would escalate and eventually become readily apparent.

With my first dog.

We moved to California in 1948. All the Andersens moved to the San Francisco Bay area, following the lead of two of Stanley's brothers, who had been stationed at the Alameda Naval Base during the war. My mother's relatives remained in Wisconsin. We exchanged pine cones for palm trees, but the move had no apparent effect on our family dynamics—except perhaps allowing my parents to worry less about contact with my birthparents. We bought our first automobile, a black 1942 Chevrolet, and set out for California in the spring of 1948. My parents left my dog in Wisconsin. As long as I have anything to say about it, no dog of mine will ever be left behind again.

Chapter Three
Biology 101

The cruelest lies are often told in silence.
—*Robert Louis Stevenson*

I learned of my position in the Andersen family at age twelve. Mother had told me about her hysterectomy (although she indicated it occurred in 1939), and I learned something about the biology of reproduction. Combining this information with my birth date in 1940 raised a major question about my birth. I asked Mother about this dilemma, which while being the obvious thing to do, might suggest the adoption issue was straightforward, open, and healthy—none of which was true. Looking back, it surprises me I did not worry about this quandary for months, which would have been more consistent with the secretive and conflictual nature of the issue. Not more than a week after becoming aware of the difficulty, I asked about it. My inquiry was not perfectly casual, but I undertook it without great hesitation. Frankly, I expected confirmation of being the

Andersens' natural child and assumed some facet of biology unknown to me would explain away the dilemma. I even formulated such a reason, thinking that perhaps the uterus functioned only in the early part of pregnancy, following which the fetus could survive elsewhere inside the mother—wishful thinking perhaps—although rare instances may have occurred where ectopic pregnancies carried to term. But considering my age, the idea supported belief. In any event, whatever the realities of fetal development, I fully expected there would be some ready biological explanation that would make everything "normal."

Mother and I were home the evening we finally broached the adoption issue. My parents no doubt worried about this event for years. Father had gone out, a necessary precondition, for on issues like this he had the sensitivity of a grenade. I recall nothing of the hours leading up this exchange, although certainly had decided to express my concern. We stood in the living room. Feeling little anxiety, but determined to resolve the issue, I asked, out of the blue, if I was adopted. "Yes," mother responded. Surprise!

Stepping on a land mine is not painful. One experiences an ill-defined awareness of dysfunction, combined with a greater or lesser degree of fear and disorientation, but no pain. One does not expect the event. This analogy most readily comes to mind in trying to describe my reaction to this discovery. My mother's words registered somewhere in my brain, and I was immediately aware of the metaphorical explosion, but I felt little pain and remained relatively unaware that a major part of my life had just been blown away. It seemed like I belonged somewhere else, that this woman was no longer my mother and the Andersens, no longer my family. I wanted to be instantaneously transported into a different family, a different town, a different existence. My life was suddenly transformed into a charade, a life being lived in exile—something to be endured until I could return to my real world where everything was not pretense and where my place in the family was more than something dictated

by the latest social theory. To this day, I have not entirely resolved these feelings. Following actual explosions, people eventually learn to walk on artificial legs and even to play basketball
on them. But they never prefer artificial legs over the real thing.
Perhaps the same is true with metaphorical explosions as well.

The shock (and the wish to be gone) lasted only a few
seconds. Quickly supplanting it was the more self-conscious
realization that I better refrain from saying or doing anything
upsetting to my mother. I did not say to myself, "Bob, you are
distressed about this, but in the interest of keeping peace around
the house, you had better feign indifference." Had I been able
to counsel myself in such a manner, the situation would have
been relatively under control. But the problem transcended mere
tactical considerations. I needed to conceal my experience not
just from my mother, but from myself as well. Having been
raised in a family that avoided adoption issues, I could not
consider a different approach. Further, experience had taught
me not to upset my mother, and I concluded that only a world-
class jerk would do so on this issue. "Crimes against humanity"
would be the level of indictment brought against me if I troubled
her on something this critical. Unfortunately, protecting Ann's
feelings meant ignoring my own. Concern about hurting my
mother, fear of moving to an orphanage, and reluctance to confront the loss of my natural family all conspired to prevent me
from acting other than how my parents had taught me: to sup-
press my feelings and ignore the adoption. I did it well, never
again speaking to my mother about the adoption.

Until recently, my most vivid recollection of that night
was of trying to protect Mother; the cover-up attained greater
conscious significance than the adoption. My adoption more
markedly affected my personality, but its effects were con-
strained to expression through unconscious channels. I now
generally distrust situations where an acceptable explanation or
outcome could be viewed as routine—i.e., situations that repeat
the mistaken assumption that my "parents" were really my

parents. Applying for a mortgage, requesting a building permit, renewing my medical license, having a dental exam, going to the veterinarian, and developing photographs comprise a few of the countless situations where rational judgment did not warrant worry, but where I expected to have problems. The fact that I can be totally unaware of issues of major importance in my life has been programmed into my brain, and I get uneasy whenever I reassure myself that my circumstances will be normal. These situations do not announce themselves as adoption related, but they can be understood as partial repetitions of the experience of learning that the Andersens were not my natural parents. One does not have to consciously recall an experience for it to have a significant impact on one's life. In fact, it usually has a greater impact if it remains unconscious. This has certainly been true in my life.

We said a few more things that night, although everything became anticlimactic after the first several moments. I must have asked what happened to my birthparents because Ann said they were killed in an automobile accident. She lied, as she always did about my adoption. Our discussion lasted two minutes, ending with my testimony that I considered her my "real" mother. I feel sick recalling this statement, which was more the product of the coercive nature of my situation than an honest expression of my experience. Some adoptees genuinely feel their adoptive mothers are their "real" mothers; but not me, certainly not then, and tragically I lacked confidence to say anything else. I dutifully renounced all interest in my biology, birthfamily, ancestry, heritage—in short, to a major part of my life—and no one questioned the absurdity of it all. I find that terribly disappointing. Are adoptees expected to take leave of their senses as well as their names?

My mother expected this one-minute composite of lies and half-truths to close forever my inquiry about the adoption. It did close it for many years. I told my best friend about the adoption, but we discussed it in a matter-of-fact manner and never spoke of it again. Neither of us knew what to do with the issue.

Father and I had an interchange about adoption in 1959. I cannot recall how we got onto the subject (we rarely discussed anything, let alone the adoption), but it related to Ann's surgery and my expressing concern that perhaps as a result of the surgery her judgment on sexual matters might be compromised. Father construed this as an assault on his masculinity, which angered him and disposed him to talk about the adoption. His intention at this point was probably not to be helpful. He said he had been told that my birthfather was a doctor and my mother a nurse. They were unmarried, of German and English descent, not killed in an automobile accident, and, as far as he knew, still alive.

While this was a great deal of information, I did nothing with it. Other than the above discussion and the one with my best friend, I did not talk about the adoption for the next twenty years. The issue of legalizing my adoption, however, remained to be settled. Custody still officially remained with my natural parents. At age fourteen I had yet to be given a name.

Robert Lawton handled the case for my parents. I talked with Mr. Lawton several times in recent years, and he felt I should not be privy to the issues that transpired between him and the Andersens. Lawton expressed reservations about discussing the case because of client confidentiality, even though at the time of our conversations one of his clients was dead and the other in diapers. I had difficulty accepting his position. Was it not, after all, my adoption? No one else in my family remained oriented for time, place, and person, and yet even at that point he would not speak openly with me. Lawton's unwillingness to help brings to mind situations where fifty-year-old adoptees need written permission from eighty-year-old adoptive parents before the state will provide nonidentifying information about the adoptee's natural parents. Situations such as this conform better with a view of adoptees as chattel rather than chosen children.

Lawton did tell me some things, although his credibility became suspect. I hoped the Andersens had told him how they obtained me. It seemed reasonable that if two people were attempting to adopt a child who had been living with them for fourteen years, the issue of how the child came to be theirs would be relevant. I asked what had been said in that respect. He told me the Andersens said nothing about it and he had not asked. His answer resembled the one my father gave me when I inquired why he and Ann delayed adopting me for fourteen years. My father had responded, "We were so happy to have you, we just didn't think of it." Was I missing something in these situations or were these just incredibly stupid answers? Lawton said he had defined his role as an advocate of the adoption, not as a district attorney. Apparently he felt a district attorney would ask such questions. Did it never cross his mind that a judge might ask them as well? I'm sure it did.

Lawton described his work on my adoption as one of the most satisfying of his career, which is surprising because handling an adoption would seem to be a rather ordinary endeavor. Taking Lawton at his word raised the question of what made this case so special. I noticed he slightly dramatized the situation when in a letter he stated, "I was the one who handled your adoption and recall vividly the circumstances giving rise to it—you were about to play Little League baseball and you were such a star that proof had to be furnished of your age!" To my recollection, my age had already been verified by the use of a baptismal certificate. I did make the all-star team, but my performance was not so outstanding as to suggest any deception about my age. Anyway, Little League is hardly high drama.

It seemed to highlight the case for Mr. Lawton that he could bend the law to fit what he considered to be a worthy cause. The law required an effort be made to contact my natural parents. No one did that. Lawton talked with the judge and convinced him I would do better to live with the Andersens. This judgment might have been correct, but state law still required that an attempt be made to contact my natural parents. Instead, they published a notice in a small northern California community and asked for a birth certificate from Illinois rather than Wisconsin. This chicanery seems to be the only thing unusual enough about my case to have made it special for the lawyer. A sample of Mr. Lawton's "work" can be found on page two of my adoption decree:

> That said child ROBERT STANLEY ANDERSEN, a minor, on or about the 18th day of April, 1940, was wholly abandoned and deserted and left at the residence of petitioners in Racine, Wisconsin by a party or parties or at the behest of the parent or parents of said minor child, without any provision or means whatsoever being made or left by said parents or either of them or at all for the identification of said child, or its parents, or either of them . . .

What a pleasant narrative! Perhaps people consider it their civic duty to lie about adoption.

Lawton told me that when the judge called the case, two people besides those in our party stood up. This horrified my parents, who feared that these people were my birthparents. Actually, their name also was Andersen, but they had come to court for a different case. He related this story, thirty years after the fact, with some amusement; but certainly no one laughed at the time.

Our family talked little about going to court. We said nothing about the adoption on the way to the hearing and nothing about it on the way back. We had no ceremony, no celebration, no congratulations. The adoption remained a taboo subject, and we pretended it didn't exist. Our suppression has affected my ability to recount the court experience (as well as other major adoption events). Had I come from a family that was open about adoption, I might be able to more completely describe our day in court. In reality, my mind remains blank for much of this event. Affects concerned me, mine and my mother's, and affects are what I recall today. I clearly remember the tension on the way to the hearing and Mother's obvious relief on the way back. But nothing registered about how the courtroom looked, who attended, what we did for the rest of the day, etc. We could have driven off the road on the way home and I would not have noticed.

My family, circa 1952.

I do recall that during the actual proceeding the judge asked me if I wished to remain with the Andersens or go to a boys' home. Incredulous! I did not view this as a real question. There was not actually much choice. But in recent years I have reflected on this inquiry many times, wanting to go back and answer it again. I do not regret choosing to remain with the

Andersens. But I do regret my way of making the decision. I made it too quickly, with little understanding and with no sense of authorship. No doubt it was better for me to live with the Andersens, but perhaps not at the expense of selling out my heritage. With some information and some courage, I could possibly have held out for both—they should not have been mutually exclusive.

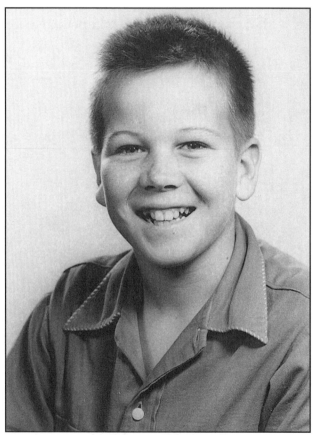

**At this age I learned
of my adoption.**

Chapter Four
Veneer

When the wayfarer whistles in the dark,
he may be disavowing his timidity, but
he does not see any the more clearly for
doing so.
—*Sigmund Freud*

My life did not immediately change upon learning of my adoption. I progressively became more screwed up, but that might have happened even without learning of the adoption. Some acute disturbance following this discovery would have provided a sign of health, but I carried on as though nothing happened. On the surface this issue appeared insignificant, but in reality its enormous importance served to prevent me from even considering it. Ignoring the adoption I became estranged from my emotions, dissociating them from any effective control. The divergence mentioned earlier between my feelings on the inside (not good) and my appearance on the outside (not bad) continued, but eventually my performance would suffer. At some point one's ability becomes subject to the person expressing it, and my person was as uncertain as my name.

Carrying on as usual meant playing sports. When the Andersens get together they talk, barbecue, and go fishing. I am uncomfortable without a ball in my hand. Although much of my life transpired on a playing field, mastery has eluded me; this book does not evolve into a story in which I strike out eighteen Dodgers en route to winning the World Series. Sports matter in my life because I most naturally pursue these activities. Seeing many adoptees reunited with their birthparents has impressed me with how closely the activities of adoptees parallel those of their natural parents. Most likely a meeting between me and my birthfather (birthmother?) would occur on a baseball diamond or a basketball court.

My athletic *curriculum vitae* reads that I earned nine high school letters, became varsity football and baseball captain, received a baseball scholarship to the University of California, played one semester of college basketball, enjoyed several years of semi-pro baseball, and finished four Boston Marathons. While this history looks good on paper, I never realized my full my potential. I played well, but not always, and inconsistency became a major problem.

I could never determine what caused my inconsistency. Having above-average ability, practicing regularly, and being in excellent shape, the problem did not appear to be physical. This left only mental aspects to consider, but that provided little help for I knew even less about psychology than physiology. Positive thinking proved useless, but then dealing with psychological factors involves more than saying nice things to yourself fifty to a hundred times a day. (It requires exploring motivation, resolving conflicts, and establishing new perspectives—all of which require a lot of time and effort.) Ignorant of the mental aspects of performance, I had reached my limit by attending solely to mechanics. But I could not consider the person behind the mechanics because doing so would have required confronting my adoption.

I thought privately about my adoption, at unguarded moments, when the subject appeared to surface by itself. Apparently I regarded thinking this way as a lesser crime than full premeditated deliberation. Being an adoptee seemed more acceptable than being an only child. My role models at this time (seventh and eighth grades) were kids from the poorer part of town, and being an only child presented me as a wimp compared to these people, who often had five or six siblings and whose parents would never be confused with Ozzie and Harriet Nelson. As an adoptee I became transformed from an only child into a child from a broken home, which made me feel more commanding. Also, I could claim the possibility of having siblings. But the sibling fantasy never brought much satisfaction, for I assumed that the salutary effect of siblings resulted more from living with them than from merely listing them on a pedigree; and my broken home involved more abstraction than reality.

I considered that Marilyn Monroe could be my sister. While perhaps imagining this about other women as well, only about Marilyn can I recall such fantasies today. While not delusional, this idea transcended idle thought. An interesting question might be why it involved Marilyn Monroe. Marilyn, of course the sex symbol of the 1950s, was not my favorite actress. Natalie Wood, co-star with James Dean in *Rebel Without A Cause* (the role model movie for anyone aspiring to move down the socioeconomic ladder), claimed that spot. Why not Natalie? Eva Marie Saint *(Raintree County)*, Ava Gardener *(On The Beach)*, and Julie Christie *(Doctor Zhivago)* played roles that moved me more than anything Marilyn did. Why not one of them? Marilyn, however, was screwed up. She came from a broken home, her life was a mess, yet despite her problems she accomplished something. I saw similarities between us and apparently found it easier to identify with her than with someone whose life was a beach. The identity issue involved more than silver-screen fantasies, for I found girls who had problems (financial, emotional, academic) more attractive than to those who did not. But I dated the "normal" (preppie) ones, which made for some long evenings with precious little of substance to share.

I developed the conviction that my natural parents were jet-setters, who left me because I was boring. Again, this belief did not derive from discussion or conscious thought. Rather, the idea simply came into existence, as if by itself. Since I was obliged to ignore my adoption (considering it granted it importance), and since the adoption issues persisted, these issues gained expression through unconscious channels—in this case by merely coming into existence, unannounced and unquestioned. Predictably, I assumed the responsibility for being abandoned— the default position for all adoptees.

Throughout these years I always worked, starting with lawn jobs at age ten and bowling pins at age twelve. Subsequently, I became a caddy, busboy, grocery clerk, maintenance man, stock clerk, and a lifeguard. I sold newspapers at football games, managed lockers at a swimming pool, cleaned a butcher shop, dug ditches, and pumped gasoline. These jobs allowed me to buy my own cars and pay my own insurance. (Auto insurance cost eighty dollars a year—people were not litigious.) I took these jobs for the money, not to prepare for a career or to learn the value of a dollar. But Stan and Ann worked very hard as well, so separating nature from nurture on this issue remains difficult.

I read little and avoided solitary activities, spending most of my time with my male friends, with whom my relationships went well. Philosophically, I defaulted to middle-of-the-road, which in the fifties meant following the crowd. Activism or sociopolitical movements found few adherents in those days. Life consisted of sock hops, friends, and Friday night football games. Everyone drove American-made cars, wore American-made clothes, and listened to American-made radios. Television was black and white; so was life. The fifties evolved much like they are now nostalgically portrayed. Ricky Nelson was just David's little brother; many years would pass before *Mary Lou* and many more before the plane crash. Conformity reigned, which for adoptees meant blending into their adoptive families. Search was not happening in the fifties. Florence Fisher may have been searching—but she did it without a support group.

Self-consciousness defined my teenage years, and few situations left me comfortable. I tried to emulate whatever looked good, but could never be more than counterfeit. Going through the motions, my life became mere simulation. I dated the girls of my choice, went to all the dances, and became king of Sadie Hawkins Week; but I had no female relationships of any substance. Nothing poignant would result from a meeting today between me and any of my high school girlfriends. I should have been forging an identity and expanding relationships, but was not. My life was just veneer and beginning to wear thin. Mercifully, high school ended before I became totally exposed.

My yearbook picture at Cal.

Chapter Five

Hard times in higher education

To make a prairie it takes a clover and one
    bee,
One clover, and a bee,
And revery.
The revery alone will do,
If bees are few.

                              —*Emily Dickinson*

My parents expressed little interest in whether I attended college. We never talked about schools, discussed careers, or addressed my academic life, not then, not ever. That was probably unusual for a family, but perhaps normal for us. After all, ours was not a normal family. When I got all A's in my senior year, Father merely questioned why some were minuses. Not displeased, he merely seemed unable to find anything more appropriate to say. I learned to keep quiet about my accomplishments. For example, I never thought to tell Father about being elected varsity football captain. Mother urged me to do so, although the information appeared to make him more uncomfortable than pleased. I informed neither of them when elected baseball captain. The Andersens did not identify with my activities. But neither did they interfere with them.

Father would have preferred that I emulate him and work at his electronics plant. He supervised a production line at Sierra Electronics, a company that made nonconsumer electrical equipment, such as marine radio transmitters and receivers. My mother worked on the assembly line at Fishers, a small electronics company that made metal detectors. College graduates could not be found in either of my parent's families, which occupationally included a machinist, a sheet metal worker, a factory foreman, a grocery clerk, a painter, a waitress, a printer, a mechanic, and numerous housewives.

The Andersens made a firm distinction between blue- and white-collar workers, and they proudly belonged to the blue-collar group. A hard-working, Democratic, pro-labor family, the Andersens did not envision an education at Berkeley to be as useful as one at the School of Hard Knocks. My mother failed to finish high school. My father did not complete grammar school. A college education eluded their experience, and they could not readily identify with my doing well academically and then attending college. In addition, the education issue highlighted our biological differences and emphasized the unusual nature of our family. Also, since the Andersens believed my natural father practiced medicine, they could almost view my going to college and majoring in premed as defecting to the enemy—although no one said anything to that effect.

It bothered me little that my parents showed minimal interest in my schooling (or other major aspects of my life, for that matter). I never really thought much about it. Had they asked questions, they would have done so merely for show, which would only have created new problems. Father and I once went to a Giants' game, not because of a mutual interest in baseball, but to foster some father-son bonding. When he characterized number 24 as minor league, I realized this togetherness stuff would not make it—Willie Mays wore 24.

We handled the Giants' game like we handled everything. Father and I went through the motions, pretending to enjoy the game, while our conversation dwindled down to occasional perfunctory remarks. Father then began patronizing me, repeatedly asking if I wanted some popcorn, a hot dog, or whatever. At age sixteen, if I wanted something, I could get it myself. His line of inquiry irritated me—I felt a bigger issue existed here than whether Father took me to the concession stand. But we were both excessively polite, and neither of us said anything. We never thought to discuss our reactions. Not surprisingly, we attended no more baseball games together.

Unwilling to confront the major issues in our relationship, my parents did better to say nothing about college. In addition, they lacked the background to ask questions about higher education. My parents could not, for example, ask whether I considered quantum mechanics an appropriate course for undergraduate study or whether quantitative analysis proved more difficult than qualitative analysis. So they asked nothing, I said nothing, and no one really noticed. Until now.

I went to college because my grades encouraged me to do so. Stanford and California-Berkeley comprised my only choices. These might seem pretentious choices, both being superior institutions, but their reputations remained largely unknown to me. Stanford provided my only first-hand contact with a university. Growing up two miles from the campus, I assumed it to be just another school—like I thought San Francisco was just another city, Santa Cruz just another beach, and Los Gatos just another place to grow grapes. These misconceptions have since been corrected.

I chose the University of California, the only school to which I applied. I chose Cal because they gave me a baseball scholarship and because I anticipated fitting in better at Berkeley than at Stanford. Stanford students came from real families. They constituted the elite of society, people from privileged homes. Perhaps they had parents who had gone to Stanford, or maybe even several generations of blood relatives preceded them. These people had roots. They knew their roots. Stanford students were wealthy, positioned, legitimate, and had real names from real, substantive families—at least I viewed them that way. I did not expect to fit well into this group. Berkeley, on the other hand, was a state school, and the state must take everyone. People could go to Cal when they were neither a Cabot nor a Lodge, a Hewlett nor a Packard. Perhaps Cal would be a place for students with broken, artificial, or tarnished families. I more readily identified with that group.

Cost never presented a major consideration, although fortunately, California would cost me nothing. Probably if I chose Stanford (and got in), my parents would have figured a way to pay for it. Actually, I paid most of my college expenses myself with money saved from part-time and summer jobs. Unfortunately, economic prudence abandoned me over the years.

I went to college hoping to gain a new family and transferred this desire to the issue of joining a fraternity, where everyone was supposed to become brothers, together, and all that good stuff. Hoping a fraternity would be like a real family, I discovered otherwise, and my year at California turned into a big disappointment. With my unrealistic expectations, albeit largely unconscious, the year could not have gone differently.

I pledged Kappa Alpha and soon wished I had not. We could boast of having an all-American quarterback (Joe Kapp), the sixth man on the national championship basketball team (Berkeley's final hour of athletic glory), and two starting varsity baseball pitchers. But only one of these heroes lived in the house. The live-ins were a group of noncelebrities, most being pretty good guys. They were not advertising or marketing majors, the types with whom I usually have nothing in common. The house should have suited me, but I envisioned belonging elsewhere—although nowhere else would have suited me any better. Being social geeks, some of my fraternity brothers embarrassed me, and in my second semester I left the house—not my finest hour.

Virginia, a friend at the sorority next door, introduced me to Mike Brennen, a friend of hers from high school who wanted to share his apartment. Mike and I hit it off well, and we became roommates. Our apartment was perfect: not expensive, yet overlooking the Golden Gate and Oakland Bay bridges. The situation worked out well and might have remained a good arrangement had I not decided to transfer out of Cal.

My baseball career bombed. Riding the pine, I wasted my year as a Golden Bear. The coach appreciated my potential but also saw my inhibitions. I could never perform to capacity. Not new for me, inhibitions had characterized my high school career as well. Potential counts for something as a high school sophomore, but a college freshman needs to produce. In sports and in other areas I could no longer flop around as a relatively big fish in a relatively small pond. Cal reflected the real world, and I showed poorly in it. The classroom remained an exception and there I could succeed. I am perhaps more capable academically than athletically. Also, since athletics mattered more to me than did academics, my neurotic problems expressed themselves more on the baseball diamond than in the chemistry lab. While not making Phi Beta Kappa, I did well in my classes.

In the summer following my year at Berkeley, I became closer friends with people from my church. Growing up as a Lutheran, our church (First Lutheran) convened outside my school district, and most of my friends had come from school. Now my world took a cosmopolitan turn. A friend's father at church put me to work at Pacific Gas & Electric, and I expanded my church activities. Virginia, my sorority friend from Cal, transferred to First Lutheran, heightening my interest in religion. Nothing beckoned me back to Cal, and Pacific Lutheran held out the promise of the communal situation I still desired. Many people from First Lutheran attended Pacific Lutheran College, and they talked highly of the school. I decided to transfer.

Perhaps Cal wasn't all bad.

Pacific Lutheran College (University) sits outside of Tacoma, Washington, a beautiful area with many activities, where the weather (except for the rain) remains excellent year round. I enjoyed Pacific Lutheran. All undergraduates lived in dormitories. While I had little in common with my fall-semester roommate, in the spring I moved in with a friend who pitched world-class softball. I pitched baseball, and the two of us often caught for each other. Roger could do more underhand with a baseball than I could do overhand, which both impressed and disturbed me. I soon picked up this softball business and within a year began pitching softball myself. Following a semester on the basketball team, I pitched varsity baseball. My last baseball game came in the league playoffs against a pitcher from Western Washington University (Ray Washburn), who went on to star for the St. Louis Cardinals. I liked everyone at Pacific Lutheran, and my sophomore year proved much better than the one at Cal. Obviously, athletics remained important.

A required study skills class directed that everyone talk personally with the professor (also the school counselor) about their academic performance. My first talk produced a second talk and eventually led to counseling. This professor introduced me to psychology, effectively enough that I changed majors to psychology. The year passed quickly, and I left Tacoma expecting to return in the fall. I planned to share an apartment with two friends, both of whom I liked and respected.

But I failed to return. My problems continued and during the summer I asked our family physician for a psychiatric referral. He sent me to an associate with whom I began a twice-a-week psychoanalytically oriented psychotherapy. This was a traditional therapy, complete with a couch, free association, a Jewish psychiatrist, and a stylish office in a fashionable part of town. My adoption remained outside the purview of this therapy, but it remained outside my thinking as well. We discussed schools and determined it would be better for me to transfer to San Jose State and continue therapy. This treatment did not resolve any major conflicts, but it provided support, and the doctor encouraged me to return to medicine. I worked as many as thirty hours a week in a machine shop while attending State. I needed the money for my psychotherapy, but operating a drill press was easier for me at this time than learning statistical variance or contemplating probability theory. The first semester at State produced my academic nadir.

My social life had improved, but recognizing the difference would have proved difficult. In high school I played a role, to the best of my ability, trying to act and feel in the socially defined manner. This meant being upbeat, happy, and confident, with a heavy emphasis on positive thinking—the attitude typically valued by teenagers. Behavior such as this works well if one's life circumstances support it, but can become awkward and contrived if one's life does not. Human beings are not free to become any kind of people they wish. The experiences of our lives determine the broad colors of these lives. We can paint a multitude of pictures within the range of colors (experience) that life gives us, but we cannot create something authentic outside our experience. People might be free to become whatever they can be, but it is hard to imagine, for example, a concentration camp survivor doing stand-up comedy or hosting a game show.

By playing less of a role and living closer to the bounds of my actual experience, I had improved my social life. While this change fostered authenticity, significance, and communication, it created its own set of problems. My life entailed being transplanted from a natural family to an unnatural one—not the life experience that lends validity to a life-is-a-beach attitude. Adoption involves loss. Adoptees, in painting the pictures that depict their lives (to stick with the metaphor), must paint in large part with the color blue—at least they must start out that way.

My strategy with women was simple and designed by default: become infatuated with someone, ask her out, hope something would happen. Women were plentiful, I asked them out, nothing much happened. It appears that I idealized certain women and felt my life would be made complete by becoming part of their world. I favored girls who resembled my idealized birthmother. I imagined my mother to be cool and self-confident and thought she left me because I was boring. My girls of choice were cool and self-confident (bordering on arrogant) and tended to be indifferent to me. My (unconscious) strategic wish in these relationships apparently concerned my abandonment and entailed proving myself worthwhile to someone who represented my birthmother. I hoped this strategy would undo the trauma of my rejection and thereby make me whole. Actually, this formula results in neurosis, as well as failure. Since the major part of my motives played out in my private world, little remained for genuine relationships. I viewed my desired girl friends as promising complete happiness, whereas I typically selected people with whom I had little or nothing in common.

Perhaps a change began in these relationships during the summer following high school graduation. With, Sheryl, a pretty high school senior, I sometimes felt sad. Feeling this way was new for me because with girls like her I usually tried to emulate a game show host. Sheryl's parents had divorced, and she lived in an apartment with her mother. Perhaps her family situation facilitated my ability to experience sadness. (Marriages lasted longer in those days, and Sheryl was my first acquaintance who lived with only one parent.) However, my "romance" with Sheryl did not last the summer, and two years passed before my involvement with Virginia.

Virginia, my friend from Cal, became my first substantive female relationship. (My male associations fared better because we shared athletics.) While Virginia and I had met at Berkeley, it took two years, following her transfer to Stanford and mine to State, before we started dating regularly. She evinced qualities that appeared lacking in me. While I floundered about, spending more time operating a drill press than attending class, Virginia attended nursing school at perhaps the best university in the country. Her father ran a junior high school in a wealthy part of Palo Alto. Virginia belonged at Stanford. Perhaps I belonged drilling holes.

What began as a whimper with Sheryl became a watershed with Virginia. Embarrassed to recall this, I remember crying frequently with Virginia. My outpouring probably helped; if one feels like crying, the advantage favors doing so—one can always try to sort it out later. But at the time I felt ridiculous. No reason presented itself for my misery. Problems punctuated my life, but my reactions appeared excessive. I was major league sad and did not know why. This was authenticity all right, but too much, too soon. Awash in authenticity and void of a conceptual framework, the whole affair became simply too embarrassing. Virginia never complained, although my outpouring must have concerned her as it did me.

Somehow our relationship ended. I remember feeling drawn elsewhere, although to nowhere else in particular. The gulf between Virginia's legitimacy and my aberrancy appeared to vast to span. We started seeing each other less often, apparently at my behest, although without any deliberate plan in mind. Had anyone formally ended the relationship, it should have been Virginia. Her parents probably applauded our separation. I never saw her much after that. Virginia now lives in Seattle, remains involved with the church, and enjoys her marriage. I learned this several years ago after writing to her. She responded, briefly recapping her life. I paid most attention to the married part.

By my senior year I acquired some stability and attended more to my studies. Having changed majors, it became necessary to complete an extra semester. By this time I excelled academically, obtaining the highest grades in physics (350 students) and quantitative analysis (85 students). Inseparable from my slide rule (remember them?), I devoted most of my time to studying. Trying to get into medical school focused my life and drew attention away from my earlier problems.

I viewed medical school as a chance to be all that I could be (i.e., the Army commercials). For me it was not an opportunity to serve mankind, do good deeds, or make money. I hoped medical school would provide an arena where I could develop personal qualities worthy of pride. While I believed my natural father practiced medicine, that belief did not consciously influence my decision to study medicine—although it must have been a factor.

Also, it appears that my roots drew me back to the midwest, influencing me to choose a school in Missouri rather than in California.   (USC, Washington University, and St. Louis University accepted me.   I did not apply to the University of Wisconsin because they accepted few out-of-state students and applying there would have appeared too obvious.) Washington University in St. Louis became my choice, in part, because of its proximity to "home."   This choice proved fortunate because Washington University its their students well and because it ranks as the fifth best medical school in the country—again, something unknown to me at the time.

In August 1963, focused on medical school and no longer terminally sad, I loaded up my 1953 Volkswagen (all medical students drove Volkswagens) and headed east to St. Louis. I had failed to consider adoption as a factor in my life and would ignore it for another twenty years. Adoption may not comprise everything in an adoptee's life—but it certainly is something. I consistently devaluated its importance.

The fraternity disappointment, my sadness with Virginia, and my academic success strike me as the most significant issues from this time period. Before leaving this chapter I would like to consider these issues and attempt to understand them in relation to my adoption. Attempting to do so is as much a political as a scientific decision, for people involved with adoption usually color their views to fit their particular needs. However, it seems more reasonable to regard adoption as a significant issue, rather than a trivial one.

My problem with the fraternity and my sadness with Virginia appear to have comprised two facets of the same problem: the abandonment by my birthfamily. Since the Andersens prevented me from thinking about the adoption, my adoption fantasies remained unconscious and unrealistic.   Joining the fraternity stimulated my unconscious wish to be united with my (idealized) birthfamily. This unrealistic expectation led to the disappointment with the fraternity and then to the sadness with Virginia. Two broad strategies are available to the adoptee in his attempt to redress his adoption experience: He can attempt to rejoin his idealized birthfamily (with the concomitant fantasy of living happily ever after), or he can attempt to adjust to the loss (both fantasized and real) of this family. My situation with the fraternity involved my wish for reunion, whereas that with Virginia involved confronting my loss. Both approaches were tumultuous, largely because I could not consciously consider my adoption. Conscious deliberation does not obviate the problems, but it does offer the adoptee some control over how, when, and where the issues are to be joined. One does better to face these problems consciously, over time, emphasizing grief as the major mode of resolution.

Finally, one should note that despite my emotional difficulties I continued successfully with my premedical studies. Perhaps this says something about genetic proclivities, if not also about identifications.

1966. My coat is synthetic.

Chapter Six
Patterns

The present contains nothing more than the past, and what is found in the effect was already in the cause.
—Henri Bergson

While the names changed the story remained the same. Psychological patterns once set in motion stay in motion unless something unusual comes along to change them. Nothing came along to change my adoption issues. I lacked an inner sense of direction, felt my natural reactions were dangerous, did not see myself as a good person, and had little sense of belonging. I seeked idealized family surrogates, did not expect things to go well, and remained conflicted toward women. My self-esteem was poor. My self-confidence, low. It sounds like a real mess. It was.

I think these feelings largely related to adoption issues. Perhaps they were really due to oedipal conflicts, or toilet training experiences, or Ann Andersen's depression, or heredity, or a lack of intestinal fortitude, or the alignment of the stars, or whatever. But I can see no reason to avoid considering them in relation to my adoption. I believe my lack of inner direction came from being assigned an identity, rather than being born into one. My instincts appeared dangerous because they set me apart and threatened the adoption cover-up. I worried about not being a good person because I could not meet my adoptive parents' expectations. I lacked a sense of belonging because I did not belong. I continued to long for an idealized family because my feelings about my natural family had been suppressed. I lost trust in the world upon discovering that the Andersens were not my parents. And I had problems with women, viewing them as prototypes of my two mothers: impractical, unavailable, exciting (birthmother); practical, available, routine (adoptive mother).

In addition, my authentic identity necessarily required considering such issues as illegitimacy, promiscuity, abandonment, and ignorance. Failing to confront these issues left me feeling fraudulent. Finally, the Andersens' lying and dissimulation complicated and exacerbated these problems. One can easily imagine that the superimposing of these issues on the exigencies of life created enough dissonance to result in significant problems.

During my final year at State, the crises of high school and early college partially subsided. My concentration improved, and I resolved two major issues in my life: I became engaged and was accepted to medical school. My fiancee, Linda, and I dated for about a year. We met in chemistry class. Linda was pretty, shy, and unlike the other girls I had dated—not Heather Homemaker nor a clone of my fantasized birthmother. Being an only child, not being especially close to her parents, and having problems of her own, Linda had some things in common with me.

Linda and I married following my freshman year in medical school. We did not marry because we had developed a deep appreciation of each other's personal qualities or because we shared important personal ambitions. We married, largely, because it was the thing to do. We probably saw ourselves as social equals, with neither of us about to win a self-confidence contest. Linda and I related to each other as we had learned to relate: We shared the business of life, but did not share personal feelings. Socially, we spent the early years of our marriage playing bridge with other medical school couples. Later we began to raise and show German Shepherds. I do not remember ever discussing my adoption with Linda. Possibly, she did not even know I was adopted.

Medical school was fun. Before you sign up, however, let me warn you that I think running marathons is fun. In fact, going to medical school and running marathons have much in common: Neither comes easily, both require enormous effort, and both require infinite time. Yet, medical school and marathons are both elective, so that while they remain strenuous and time consuming, neither quite resembles work. Medical school can bury you. It demands most of your time. For weekend fun I caught up on items missed during the week or read elective rather than required material. Still, medical school provides adventure more than hardship—and no one forces you to do it. The studying gets tedious, but everyone is doing it with you. Cooped up studying on a pleasant Sunday afternoon, your friends will not have deserted you for the beach. Your friends will be doing just what you are doing—studying.

I did all right academically. Nothing is conceptually baffling about medical school. If you can handle college chemistry and physics, you have the capacity to master medicine. Much of medical school entails memorization, and while intelligence makes this kind of work easier, discipline gets it done. Probably anyone can learn gross anatomy if he or she studies hard enough. Not just anyone can learn differential equations. But then medical school does not require differential equations— medical school is not rocket science. Medical students must learn volumes of material. Learning it usually entails just putting one foot ahead of the other, but there is an incredible number of steps. I kept pace with my class, from the beginning to the end, right in the middle of the pack.

Medical school jocks, 1967. I'm second from left in back row.

Athletics remained a big part of my life. During my freshman year I lived in a dormitory that had a gymnasium on the first floor. Contrary to what you might believe, medical students are not just bookworms who can do little but memorize nerve tracts and compute acid-base equations. Our class had many good athletes, and the gym never suffered from lack of use. We had an intramural basketball team and lost only to the physical education majors. This loss served to show our good sense because these phys ed majors were all middle linebacker types who played basketball with the finesse of draft horses. We did have our priorities. Winning wasn't everything.

During these years adoption events *per se* were rare. My birthmother did not walk into my anatomy class and tell me I was her son, nor a sister track me down and ask for one of my kidneys. The big events (being given up, going to the Andersens, finding out, going to court, etc.) happened many years before. The important part of my story at this point concerns consequences, not events—i.e., how the adoption affected the person I had become. The relationship between the two is cloudy and necessarily involves conjecture. But I believe my adoption colored every aspect of my existence. For example, during my freshman year I joined a city softball team. I pitched well by then and played in one of the area's better leagues. Johnny Mac's Sporting Goods sponsored our team. Being the area's foremost supplier of team uniforms, Johnny Mac outfitted us with the best: white pants with black and kelly green trim, and black shirts with white and kelly green trim. One night, in full sartorial splendor, I returned to the medical school dormitory. Walking through the door, I encountered the dorm residents from my class having a meeting. I immediately felt embarrassed and out of place. Why had I forgotten about this meeting? What was I doing messing around in a softball league when everyone else was doing what was really important? I feared that in the process of doing my own thing I would stray from the group and imperil my medical career.

Actually, the meeting was unimportant. It concerned political, rather than medical issues; missing it was not like cutting class. It never occurred to me upon entering the dorm that I might feel good about being a starting pitcher on a fast-pitch softball team in perhaps the best league in St. Louis. I should have felt good about my pitching; after all, pitching softball does not logically preclude the study of medicine. I chastised myself for overlooking this meeting when in fact I would choose a game over a political meeting every time—some things come more naturally to me than others. It is probably genetic. I trusted little in following what seemed natural to me. Seeing myself as different always carried a negative connotation. Authenticity, spontaneity, and genuineness were probably associated in my mind with my natural family and therefore became feelings to be disavowed. I often tried to emulate others, but would have done better being myself. The softball example illustrates a feeling that constituted a regular component of my daily experience. Examples would be limitless.

Medical students at Washington University resembled Stanford students. They generally came from families of position. My roommate hailed from Muskogee, Oklahoma, where his family, among other things, raised and raced quarter horses on their family ranch. I once visited their place, his father flying us to Oklahoma and back in a company plane. It was hard to avoid comparing our lives. My family history included illegitimacy, abandonment, and deceit, whereas Dave's involved success, position, and identity. Dave took pride in his heritage. I hid from mine. I tried to compensate for my tarnished legacy through athletic or academic accomplishments, but was simply not that gifted.

Linda and I married in June 1964. Not having completed her chemistry degree, she started working as a lab assistant at the medical school and enrolled in night classes at Washington University. Both of us stayed very busy. At first we got along well. Each of us liked animals, so we got a dog. We followed this with a second dog, and then a third. The dogs remained pets, but for a while we showed them. We also raised a couple of litters. Initially our interests coincided, but that would eventually change.

Late in my freshman year I spoke to a psychiatry instructor about the advisability of entering psychotherapy. I do not remember what bothered me and cannot recall a precipitating event; my chronic anxiety and low self-esteem probably prompted the visit. Washington University's Psychiatry Department stressed psychopharmacology over psychotherapy, so I contacted the St. Louis Psychoanalytic Foundation, where I saw a psychiatrist two or three times. He suggested psychoanalysis. I deferred the issue, feeling better just for having contacted someone.

A year or so later, however, I decided to enter psychoanalysis. A softball game precipitated this decision. I usually practiced pitching three or four times a week. One can become rather good throwing this often, and by then the coach considered me Johnny Mac's number one pitcher. Playing in a Memorial Day tournament, we expected to win the first game, so the coach saved me for the second. We got into trouble during the first game, and I was brought in to relieve. Bad move. We won the game, but no thanks to me. I let in four runs, getting the final out on a bases-loaded, 250-foot line drive that our left fielder caught against the outfield fence. I should have handled this team with ease, but did not. All my practice and all my training did not significantly enhance my performance. Psychological issues obviously limited my ability, and I was sick of it. The time had come to do something. Maybe psychoanalysis could help. It couldn't hurt.

I entered psychoanalysis during my junior year. Linda did not complain about this, although the analysis sorely strained our budget. (As an extern one summer, my whole day's wages covered only one analytic session.) I attended sessions four times a week and did so for more than five years. The analysis spanned my last two years of medical school, my internship, and two years of residency. While the Psychoanalytic Foundation was only two blocks from the medical school, it amazes me that I could have fit all these hours into my medical schedules.

I cannot say anything good about this psychoanalytic experience. It resolved nothing and changed me little. We rarely talked about my adoption in this analysis, although we talked about everything else. My analyst understood my adoption on the basis of one assumption: The Andersens were psychologically the "real" parents and one could therefore substitute adoptive for natural and consider my psychology to be like that of everyone else. He did not consider my adoption intrinsically important. I now view this approach to be like trying to understand post-traumatic stress disorder in a Vietnam veteran without ever discussing Vietnam, or in a rape victim without ever discussing rape.

While I see myself as unchanged by this procedure, one could hardly overstate the importance it had for me at the time. I walked out of medical school lectures to go to this analysis, paid people to cover my emergency room duties in order to attend sessions, and on one occasion, when my car broke down en route to a visit, I ran four miles just to make the last fifteen minutes of an appointment. This was disease, folks, not diligence.

As a treatment method, psychoanalysis is supposed to act like a lightening rod, attracting neurotic unconscious wishes into therapy where they can be identified, understood, and resolved. The lightening rod part worked fine, but the resolution part did not. I invested this analysis with a reedition of my wish to join an idealized birthfamily. I hoped to work hard, prove myself worthwhile, become a psychoanalyst, and join the "family" of the psychoanalytic community. This scenario did not happen. The analysis perhaps provided support in that I believed something good would result from it; but the process was all being done with mirrors, and in the end I gained little from this expensive procedure.

Linda and I began to drift apart. Early in our marriage depression beset us equally. Now, with my analytic mirrors and my medical school success, I felt somewhat better, and we fell out of emotional balance. For her own reasons, and perhaps because of my encouragement, Linda also entered psychoanalysis. We never shared our analytic experiences, which is unfortunate because doing so might have helped our marriage. In some ways we got along well. We rarely argued, both liked our dogs, and each of us did our share of household chores. When I graduated from medical school, Linda transferred to Monsanto. While an intern, I adored some of the nurses at the hospital, but refrained from any involvement with them. Linda did get involved with a colleague at Monsanto. Five years after our marriage, Linda moved in with her new friend. She did not want a divorce; she just wanted a separation. The year was 1969, a time when people experimented with relationships, but it made little sense to keep our marriage together.

Splitting up did not especially upset me; divorce would allow me to pursue some of the nurses. Also, I thought Linda's leaving had more to do with her psychoanalysis than with me—that she was acting out intrapsychic conflicts stirred up by her analysis. (Common sense often yields to psychological theory.) Linda left, in part, for intrapsychic reasons. But she also left because of me. My tendency to idealize other women probably constituted my chief contribution to our divorce. I did not pursue these other women, but my spouse must have perceived the effects of my adulation of some of these people. I do not know if over the long haul Linda and I could have put it together. She broke up with her Monsanto boyfriend and transferred to Chicago. Unfortunately, we severed all contact. She took one dog. I took two. I fantasize that if Linda and I ever met again, Geisha, the dog she took, would still be alive. Geisha would be twenty-two years old! My fantasy perhaps implies that I have some unresolved feelings about our divorce—or about losing Geisha.

My work continued well. I took a medical-surgical internship, but chose to specialize in psychiatry. Internal medicine would have been my second choice. I chose psychiatry because I had invested a considerable amount of effort trying to understand psychodynamics and because I idealized psychoanalysis. At times I regret not going into internal medicine. Internists do typical doctor things. Psychiatrists do not. Psychoanalysis diverges so far from medicine that a medical education becomes virtually irrelevant. I probably made a good choice specializing in psychiatry, not for reasons envisioned at the time, but for reasons that have turned up since. Early in my psychiatric career I hoped to find family in the psychoanalytic community—as I hoped to find family in the fraternity at Berkeley. Family never happened, although I did learn some psychoanalysis. But I am not a psychoanalyst today. In fact, I never profited one penny from my six years (nearly 6,000 hours) of analytic training. I now practice general psychiatry. I like my work, although it does not confer the most prestige in the medical community. But as a psychiatrist I am better positioned to consider the psychology of adoption. I am probably better off dealing with adoption issues than treating pulmonary emboli or myocardial infarctions.

At times I become curious about what happened to Linda, but have never seriously tried to locate her. She probably remarried and therefore changed her name. Her parents, if alive, no longer reside in Fullerton. The telephone directory does not list her in Chicago under her maiden name. My second ex-wife now also works for Monsanto, at their world headquarters. I could ask her if the company has any records on Linda. Tacky?

Chapter Seven

Patterns II

We had seen the light at the end of the tunnel,
and it was out.

—*John C. Clancy*

Patterns II in many ways repeats the previous chapter. It contains another marriage, another analysis, another divorce. There are few actual adoption events, although no lack of adoption consequences and difficulties. Obviously this story could use a hero, but instead we watch me bumble from one bad marriage to another and from one analysis to another. Help eventually arrives—in the form of insight about the importance of adoption as a factor in my life—but this help remains ten years away, although some good things begin to happen in less than ten years.

I remarried three years after Linda and I divorced. My second wife, Margaret, taught elementary school music. She was twenty-five. I had turned thirty. Margaret had once been engaged to a teacher she met during a year of college in Austria, but had never married. My analyst seemed to like Margaret, and he attributed my reservations about her to my psychopathology rather than to reality. I was inclined to listen to him, since I did not value my own assessments. (Not much to cheer about here.)

Margaret and I had dated about a year when she became pregnant, an event without which we might never have married. If I had been looking for someone with qualities different from Linda, I found her. Margaret was not depressed and stayed close to her family—a plus. As a minus, also unlike Linda, she avoided work and assumed little responsibility. Her lack of responsibility proved to be a big liability, although at the time I considered her fun loving rather than irresponsible.

In 1971, soon after we married, I entered the Air Force. The United States still remained in Vietnam. Washington needed physicians, and they inducted most male medical graduates into military service. The big question for men from my medical school graduating class had been whether this duty would be as a general medical officer (i.e., probably in Vietnam) or a specialist (perhaps not in Vietnam). The military apparently determined assignments by lottery, and my number allowed me to defer enlistment until after my residency. Entering the service did not notably change our lives because the Pentagon assigned me to Scott Air Force Base, which is only thirty miles outside of St. Louis. I wore Air Force blue to work every day, but the rest of our life remained unaffected.

The Air Force treated me well. While Scott is close to St. Louis, it remains in the country. Cornfields flourished adjacent to our subdivision, miles of them, which provided an interesting change for someone from suburbia. Scott proved a pleasant place to live. The people were friendly and the work interesting. Being an Air Force Major gave me the opportunity to do special things, such as work on the flight line and interview returning prisoners of war. Scott also had plenty of athletic activities. I played squadron football, base softball, and regularly joined basketball games at lunch hour. For a person like me, my work situation could not have been better. Except for our miserable marriage, my time in the Air Force went just fine. It should be noted that no one raised a question about my right to belong in the United States military. My family disowned me, and no state acknowledged my birth; but my country claimed me. I was at least an American, if nothing else.

Early in my Air Force tour I decided to become a psychoanalyst. My decision required, among other things, that I undergo psychoanalysis with a training analyst. Although I had been in analysis for five years, it was not with a training analyst, and in part to make this shift, I stopped my first analysis. While in the Air Force, I drove early every morning to St. Louis to undertake this training analysis. To call it a training analysis, rather than a therapeutic analysis, is not entirely correct—it was both. This analysis differed from my first one in being more emotional and less intellectual. As a result of this second analytic experience, I became less depressed and developed a greater understanding of the complexity of emotional conflict. This analysis did not alter the course of my life, but it guided me in the right direction.

Amazingly, neither analysis dealt with my adoption. In all the years I was encouraged to say whatever crossed my mind, which I dutifully tried to do, the adoption never came up. In all the years my analysts attempted to read between the lines and consider the omissions, they never asked about my adoption. How could an issue of such importance remain outside the purview of a procedure designed primarily to uncover such issues? I did not consciously avoid the subject. Apparently, I unconsciously presumed that my adoption entailed matters forbidden even for psychoanalysis—which demonstrates the great intensity of my inhibitions. I did not have the courage to face my adoption, and my analysts lacked the knowledge to consider it important.

My parents occasionally visited during these years (the early seventies), and during a conversation Father once said that as an adoptive parent he always exceeded his parental require-

ments. The statement pleased him, but to me it merely emphasized the difference between adoptive and natural parents—
meeting requirements hardly seemed relevant to the way natural
parents related to their children. I have no idea how this discussion got started. It certainly did not reflect a change in the
closed attitude our family took toward adoption.

During these years, I rarely gave conscious consideration
to any aspect of being adopted. I did not wonder about my
natural parents, did not contemplate searching, and had no
questions to ask my adoptive parents. Margaret and I had two
children, and neither birth stimulated any concerns about roots,
ancestry, or family medical history. Consciously, my adoption
hardly existed.

Our marriage started badly and went downhill from
there. Margaret felt I owed her something because of the pregnancy. We related poorly and apparently chose each other for
neurotic reasons. I needed to work hard to prove myself worthwhile, while Margaret hardly worked and developed an entitle-
ment mentality. Since I was a doctor, she felt I should be able to
do everything. I tired of doing everything and resented her lack
of responsibility. She complained about everything, from the
color I painted our patio to my lack of support for her breast-
feeding ordeal. For several years I took her criticisms seriously.
Typically, I had seen myself as the cause of problems in
relationships; after all, I had posed a problem for people from the
moment of my conception. Finally, however, I could no longer
remain a scapegoat. Everything would not forever be blamed on
me. I took a stand: I moved out. For many years I considered
this my finest hour.

My finest hour did not merely entail leaving a disgrun-
tled wife. Leaving Margaret also symbolically involved confronting the effects of my adoption. I was beginning to see adoption
as it really was and not especially liking the view. The National
Committee for Adoption ran an advertisement in 1982 referring
to illegitimate children as problems: "If you're pregnant and

faced with a decision about possible solutions to your problem, call us in confidence. . . ." The Committee inserted the word *problem* in the advertisement as a substitute for the term *unwanted child*, which had drawn criticism in a previous edition. If an organization such as this stumbles all over itself trying to find a nonpejorative way to refer to adoptees, what does that say about how adoptees are viewed, at least in part, by society in general? We are unwanted at worst and remain problems at our euphemistic best. The time had come for me to stop blowing sunshine at my adoption.

I had presented problems for my birthparents and adoptive parents, but not necessarily for everyone. Perhaps other people also incurred relationship responsibilities. For the first time in my life, I realized that my emotions occurred in conjunction with situations. I was unhappy in my marriage not because my character was warped, but because nothing in the marriage made me happy. The situation did not call for a doubling of effort or three more years of psychoanalysis. It required me to cut my losses and get out. Perhaps I was, after all, a normal person reacting to an abnormal situation, rather than an abnormal person screwing everything up.

My children, Paul and Erika, were four and three when I moved out. Margaret received custody, but I obtained liberal visitation rights. I always took the children on my custody days. Paul now lives with me when not at college. Erika resides with her mother. At age twelve Erika began to embrace her mother's ideas, viewing me as the sole source of accountability in our relationship. Her attitude encroached on my newly emerging adoption issues, resulting in the two of us suspending contact for several years. We see each other more often now, but problems remain. My children appear unruffled that their father is an adoptee. Both say they have more interest in my (their) natural relatives than in my adoptive relatives.

While Paul and Erika may discount my adoption, it matters to me that I pass on no family traditions, customs, or beliefs to my children. On my side of their family there are no approaches to life, learned and proven valuable by our ancestors, that we can follow—at least none we know about. On my side of their family, I am always walking point: getting lost, wandering into traps, stepping on mines, and learning from mistakes—but never following footsteps or signposts. No tradition hallows our halls; no veterans swell our ranks. Groups like this fare poorly in combat.

Erika Andersen.

Paul Andersen.

Chapter Eight

Until death do us part

No house should ever be *on* any hill or *on* anything. It should be of the hill, belonging to it, so hill and house could live together each the happier for the other.

—*Frank Lloyd Wright*

My adoptive mother died on December 29, 1981, at age sixty-seven. Two months earlier Father had called to tell me Mother was ill. She had lost weight, was anemic, and had a mass in her abdomen. Her doctor scheduled her to enter the hospital for additional tests. I immediately flew to California.

At 3 A.M., somewhat unannounced, I called my parents from a local gas station. Unsure my presence would be welcomed, I would not have been surprised if they had told me to go back to St. Louis. It felt strange to anticipate being sent home. Something was obviously wrong when a son visiting his dying mother felt he was intruding. I anticipated the Andersens would be closing ranks in this time of crisis. Pretenses would be dropped and they might view me as an outsider. While I recall my feelings about this event more clearly than usual, such feelings were probably common.

The adoption came up in my thinking six months before my trip to California. Mother had called about a problem Father developed with his driving, and our conversation somehow shifted to their finances. Overhearing our discussion, Father grumbled in the background that because they told me about their bank balance I would want to borrow some money. He had no basis to make such a statement and it irritated me. I began to think that perhaps the adoption colored our relationship for I could not attribute his statement to my character or financial history. Thinking about the adoption was also consistent with my efforts to understand relationships on the basis of situations rather than personalities. By considering my adoption I probably disposed myself to expect a less-than-cordial welcome.

My parents did not tell me to go home. In fact, they greeted me warmly. They were obviously not doing well. Father had aged dramatically and he also appeared ill. Mother did not even get up that night. She had lost weight and suffered some pain, although she remained mentally alert and relatively cheerful. I felt sad about their situation. Also, true to character, I felt guilty about it, thinking that perhaps by visiting them more often I could have intervened before things became so dire. My old style of thinking clashed with the new. In the past I had been dutiful and self-sacrificing, but also depressed, guilt-ridden, and ineffectual. Recently, however, I assumed less responsibility for others and paid more attention to myself, but had become more effective and less depressed. I went to bed that morning not knowing which manner of thinking would prevail and hoping not to revert to my old way of thinking. It was important I remain functional. I fell asleep only because it was almost daybreak.

Fortunately, I awoke free of major self-recrimination. Mother and I had a long and pleasant conversation that day, something we regrettably had not been able to do more often in the past. It was not a sad conversation, although both of us knew it might be our last. We talked as if on a holiday visit, although in a way we had rarely done before. We never would have had this conversation had I felt responsible for her illness. I was trying to do less for her, but it was working out better for us both.

We did not talk about my adoption, which was unfortunate because Mother would have been my best source of information. Her memory remained intact, and she cared more about my interests than anyone else who knew my history. In subsequent years I often talked with my father about the adoption, but he told me as little as possible. He apparently derived a self-righteous, perverse satisfaction from carrying my life history to his grave. Not surprisingly, the two of us were never close.

I could no more have brought up the adoption at this time with my mother than I could have poisoned her coffee. Retrospectively, I appear to have lost my best chance to learn about my past, but at the time it simply never occurred to talk with her about it. I had been thinking about the adoption in an attempt to understand my relationship with my parents, but had not yet become consciously interested in my birthfamily. At the time, I would have viewed it as an egregiously callous and self-centered act to ask my dying mother about my natural family. Today, in the same situation, I probably would ask her.

The next day Mother entered the hospital, where she quickly deteriorated. I did not remain with her during her hospitalization but, instead, shuttled back and forth between St. Louis and Palo Alto. She was found to have renal cancer, which proved to be metastatic and inoperable. Efforts at palliative treatment accomplished little. Mother and I never talked again, other than about the daily issues of her management. We placed her in a convalescent home where she died two weeks later. I clearly remember my last visit to the convalescent home. She felt I should get back to my children and my work. We had said all we intended to say. It was time to go, but I knew we would never meet again. I must have started to leave ten times before finally doing so. We said goodbye. I stood up and walked out. Reason prevailed over emotion, but that fact provided little satisfaction. Mother died one week later.

While being sad about my mother's death, I was also angry, probably at her. Mother was the major reason I had been forbidden to think about my biological roots. Although she physically treated me well, she had nevertheless been an active party to the deceit and lies surrounding my adoption. Our interests on that issue had clashed, and perhaps she, as did my father, saw me as without rights in the matter—a second-class citizen because of my illegitimacy. In the years since her death, I have come to view Ann Andersen less and less as my mother. How I think about her today depends on how I imagine she would have reacted to my interest in my heritage. If I imagine her as supportive of this interest, I view her as my mother. But if I think of her as opposed to it, she becomes something else. I cannot conceive of someone being a mother and not being supportive of her child's interest in such a major issue.

During my mother's illness, Aunt Shirley called to express her sympathy. She was the youngest of my father's siblings, not many years older than myself. The two of us had always related well. Shirley went on to discuss the health problems in the Andersen family and indicated I was fortunate not to be a member of the family (referring to my different genetic background). I responded that not being a member of the family I did not entirely feel like a member of the family. Shirley said she did not understand why I felt that way, since my parents had always loved me. (She had just referred to me as not being an Andersen. Was I supposed to feel like an Andersen when the family viewed me otherwise?) Shirley's statement exemplifies the problems in logic that often permeate adoptions. Is love supposed to eradicate biology?

Several weeks after my mother's death, I met Barbara, a woman who for a year became a major part of my life. We made an unlikely pair, but that did not impede what was for a time a special relationship. That the relationship began so soon after my mother's death was probably more than coincidence. My mother had usually become upset whenever I showed enthusiasm for someone other than her, perhaps reflecting an insecurity that I would one day abandon her for my birthmother. Following Mother's death, I became more tolerant of my reactions. Candor and honesty began to overshadow duty and responsibility. Given the situation, if I had not fallen in love with Barbara, I probably would have found someone else. (Analysis sometimes takes the charm out of relationships.)

While my emphasis might have been more on process than content, Barbara did have her special qualities. She was a stylish, attractive, vivacious woman who traveled on a relatively fast track. Barbara had recently separated from her second husband, a successful sales representative, often mistaken for Burt Reynolds. They had resided in one of the finer parts of town, and entertaining two or three times a week, often by their pool, had been a regular part of her routine. Barbara was quick-witted, funny, hard-working and a devoted mother of two children.

Her life had not always entailed pools and parties. For good reason she ran away from home at age fourteen, whereupon she moved to Hollywood and began a career as a beautician. Some of her clients had been movie stars, and her first husband directed motion pictures. Education had not played a major part of her life, but a lack of schooling did not prevent her from obtaining a management position with a beauty supply company. Barbara had serious health problems, mainly with her back.   Also, she tended to be impulsive, opinionated, and sarcastic.

Barbara became the most significant romantic involvement of my life. Other relationships and romances have followed, but this one remains unique. Barbara resembled a first love. One could not overstate the emotional importance she had for me at the time. I would not want to have missed this relationship—nor would I want to repeat it.

We met at a night club. Equinox, the resident band, had just begun a Fleetwood Mac medley that usually forced me onto the dance floor. (Oh, to be young again!) Looking for a partner, I noticed Barbara sitting pensively at a table. She was cute, petite, and looked younger than her actual age. I did not imagine the two of us would have much in common, but the music beckoned and I expected we could at least coexist on the dance floor for the next ten minutes. We stayed longer than ten minutes. I failed to notice how pretty she was until we were together. It was hard to get the sight and feel of her out of my mind—I tried.

Barbara essentially initiated our relationship. I viewed us as too improbable, whereas she overlooked our differences. It escapes me what interested her in me, for her prototypical boyfriend sold cars, partied several times a week, and might be mistaken for Robert Redford or Tom Selleck. Apparently she also favored process over content at this time in her life. Having recently left her husband and contemplating a career change, Barbara faced some hard financial decisions. Maybe because I practiced medicine and considered her interests, she found some security in our relationship. As individuals we differed markedly. Barbara loved the nights, while I savored the days. Opposites may attract, but that attraction does not stop the sun from rising and setting.

Although we obviously differed, we also shared some personal characteristics: We both carried problematic pasts, took our work seriously, and remained absorbed with our children.

More important for our relationship, we could talk, something she could not do with her prototypical boyfriends. I had reservations about getting involved, but they faded with time. Barbara's many physical problems concerned me, as did our differences in style.

Barbara's back was an orthopedic nightmare. While she handled her symptoms with dignity, I feared that some day these symptoms would depress her, and people would expect me to assuage her distress. The Andersens had once called upon me to sacrifice my heritage in compensation for Ann Andersen's loss of reproductive capacity. That endeavor did not prove satisfying or worthwhile, and I hesitated at volunteering for similar duty. While I enjoy being helpful, I do not enjoy having other people's responsibilities shifted entirely to me, as happened with my mother's sterility; and I do not appreciate sacrifice being labeled something else. Finally, with Barbara's history and her current marital situation, one had to question her capacity for involvement. My psychoanalytic colleagues would have considered her an improbable candidate for a long-term relationship. Conventional wisdom advised me to get out; everything else urged me to continue.

The energy in my brain at that period flowed from left to right. It was a time to increase attention to subjective, affectual cues and decrease it to probability theory and standards of responsibility. I experienced Barbara as a loving, considerate person, and that sufficed for me—someone else could figure out how she got to be that way. She made it easy to resolve my concerns and we progressively became more involved. At its best, our relationship entailed togetherness, belonging, and a sense of beating the odds. I had been in love before and together before, but never both in love and together with the same person before.

The relationship eventually collapsed under the sheer weight of our differences. Barbara led the way into our relationship, and she led the way out of it. She left, in part, to pursue a relationship with her new boss. I was incredibly sad when we parted and made no effort to feel otherwise. Having entered this relationship by following my feelings, I intended to exit the same way. Getting over Barbara took months, but eventually it happened. Our relationship sparkled while it lasted. I have no regrets about our year together.

At the possible expense of wistfulness, I would like to consider a psychodynamic formulation of this relationship. One should note several things: (1) Barbara came along three weeks after my mother's death. (2) She closely fit the prototype of my birthmother image. (3) I felt more intensely for her than for my previous romances. (4) The relationship entailed togetherness, improbability, and belonging—feelings that also might apply to a relationship with my birthmother. Was this all coincidence? Probably not. My adoptive mother's death apparently allowed me to experience feelings for my birthmother, feelings long repressed, which, in part, found expression with Barbara.

My feelings for Barbara were partially due to transference. Transference is a psychoanalytic term that refers to the tendency for people to unconsciously transfer feelings and attitudes from past relationships onto people in present relationships. While not exclusively a psychoanalytic concept, analysts coined the term, study the issue the most, and emphasize the unconscious aspect of the process. People generally transfer feelings and attitudes from past conflictual relationships, the memories of which have been repressed. Transference parallels the precept in history that those who do not remember the past are destined to repeat it. We do not transfer feelings we remember. We do not fully remember relationships from which we transfer feelings. Transference sits as a way station between remembering and repeating. Psychoanalysts encourage the experience and expression of transference in the therapeutic situation as a step toward the conscious recollection of repressed memories. Working with the transference provides the cornerstone of psychoanalysis; without it, psychoanalysis would cease to exist.

We all relate to others, in part, on the basis of transference. The degree of transference depends on how problematic our pasts have been and how much of those pasts have been repressed. Everyone, for example, to some degree views the President of the United States as a father figure. But not everyone falls in love with a movie star and tries to kill the President to prove his love. While both are examples of transference, one is obviously more extreme. In general, the greater the component of transference in a relationship, the more difficult that relationship is likely to be. In psychoanalysis, under controlled conditions, transference becomes a useful therapeutic tool. In the real world transference often screws things up.

Transference occurs more frequently when the person in the present resembles the image of the person from the past. Repressed hatred from a relationship with an authoritarian father will more likely be experienced toward a police officer than a circus clown. Unrequited childhood love will be more easily rekindled by the average beauty contestant than the average bag lady. The mothers of our childhoods were all beautiful, the fathers were all strong, and the people of our transferences are likely to be the same.

Upon my mother's death I could apparently more freely experience my emotions, but not so fully that I immediately considered my birthmother. Barbara became a first step along the way. At times during our relationship I remember wanting Barbara as my mother rather than my girlfriend, for as her son we would be bound together for life. This wish, however, always embarrassed more than enlightened me. During our year together I thought of Barbara as Barbara, not as a birthmother substitute, although throughout our relationship I always puzzled about the two of us.

Following our breakup, my sadness gradually transformed from missing Barbara to missing my birthmother. At some point the shift became complete. In grieving the loss of Barbara, I apparently also began to grieve the loss of my birthmother. Doing so lifted some of the repression, allowing me for the first time in my life to think about the woman who brought me into existence. Isn't life great?

Ann K. Andersen (1914-1981).

Chapter Nine

I am, therefore I search

The only paradise is paradise lost.
—*Marcel Proust*

"Out of sight, out of mind" is not an aphorism coined by a birthmother or adoptee. One should amend it to exclude first-order relatives. I had never seen my natural relatives, but that fact did not diminish their significance. The more I thought about them, the more important they became. I began to realize that my birthparents were more than abstract concepts or dirty words. They were, in fact, real people who had themselves been part of real families. Each had parents and, probably, brothers and sisters (my grandparents, uncles, and aunts!). A history accompanied each of these families—abilities, liabilities, tendencies, and traditions (as well as a name) passed on throughout the generations. Their blood is my blood. Their blood is my children's blood. These people gave us our heritage. All the laws and all the love in the world would not alter that fact. My parents had a story about their involvement and an epilogue to that story. I had questions about both. Was my mother glad she gave me up? Did she ever regret her decision? What did my parents look like? What did they do? What kind of people were they? Do I have brothers and sisters? I had many questions. Why shouldn't I?

Not all adoptees search. But all adoptees who think much about their natural relatives eventually must decide if they will look for them. Today, those who look usually find. Years ago, they did not. Some people see adoptee search as a sign of psychopathology. They reason that if an adoptive family accepts and loves their adoptive child he will have no need to seek his natural family. Others, myself included, view search as a sign of health. We reason that an adoptee raised in an atmosphere of honesty and love will more naturally express an interest in this important part of his life. People jealously guard their differences of opinion, which probably reflect their biases toward one or the other corners of the adoption triangle. Because professionals "working" for adoptive parents produced most of the early adoption writing, the preponderance of initial opinion described search as unhealthy. Today, as more adoptees and birthparents make their views known, people are beginning to see search as a sign of health. I have published two papers on searching, and they reflect opinions gaining increasing acceptance. The papers state: (1) A more important question than why adoptees search is why they do not. (2) Search provides a useful activity for the adoptee en route to developing an authentic sense of self, but its value can be overstated. The title "I am, therefore I search" assumes a slight poetic excess. The statement "I search, therefore I am" assumes a greater therapeutic excess.

An adoptee friend of mine began to look for her birthfamily and fortunately shared her experience with me. She told me about a new search group in St. Louis. Had she informed me of such a group several years earlier, I would have given it little thought; but at this time the group intrigued me. I decided to attend, albeit armed with the defense that I was merely curious and not really planning to search—this all still remained dangerously seditious stuff.

The group (ALMA—Adoptee Liberty Movement Association) met monthly. It had about forty members when I joined. Being a new group, most members remained actively involved in their personal searches. Our ALMA chapter decreased in size over the years. Seven years ago, fifteen to twenty people came to meetings. Today, only about five people attend, and the group meets only irregularly. Usually a member finds his or her family in less than a year. People drop out of our ALMA chapter after they find. That they do not continue after finding their families says two things about the group: (1) It provides good search assistance. (2) It provides poor emotional support.

Many adoptees initially attended ALMA citing curiosity as their motive, but before long everyone began to search. We intellectualized our reasons for searching. I pretended an interest in broadening my professional understanding of adoptee psychology. Others stated they simply wanted to complete genealogical charts. Many claimed only to be seeking medical information. While these intellectual reasons provided our tickets for admission, emotional reasons supplied the real impetus to search. Most members of our group ultimately wanted to see, touch, and talk to their mothers, fathers, sisters, and brothers. Who wouldn't?

I cannot discuss the initial part of my search without talking about the search group. Initially, the group assumed more importance than my actual search. Feelings about my birthparents, long suppressed and repressed, did not just pop up one day along with the morning toast. Instead, they entered consciousness in tentative and disguised ways, often via transference. Although these feelings belonged to the past, they were crystallized by the present. I could, for example, feel closer to

Sheri, an adoptee with whom I could talk, than to my birth-mother, whom I had never met. My feelings may not have been as appropriate toward Sheri as to my birthmother, but without Sheri I might not have experienced anything at all. Many of us related in large part on the basis of transferred feelings. Trans-ference was the least understood, yet perhaps the most impor-tant, factor determining how we functioned as a group.

Some group members undoubtedly acted on the basis of transference. Dean, whom I had never met before, waited in the parking lot to pick a fight with me because I failed to answer a psychiatric question to his satisfaction. Marsha had the water turned off to my house because I did not meet her for a drink following an adoption conference. Two weeks after we met, I wrote a note to Karen, a woman half my age, telling her I loved her. Julie called me every day for two months after we spent an evening together.

Following official meetings, our group gathered at a local pub, where some of us would talk about adoption above the table while planning the rest of the evening below it. If this sounds like a soap opera, it was, and unfortunately this was the good part. The bad part was the leadership's obeisance to rules and regulations. For example, on one occasion a hospital sent me the name and address of one of our member's birthmothers, but our group leader would not give me the adoptee's phone number because he wasn't supposed to give out numbers. The same leader barred a birthmother from attending ALMA meetings because she planed to organize a birthparents' group. (Five birthmothers walked out of this meeting and never returned.) New members could not get search information until they paid their forty dollar (now sixty dollar) membership fee, a restriction that prevented some from continuing. The group officials toler-ated angry expressions about adoption, but certainly never appreciated them or learned from them. The leader told lies for political expedience, and, for reasons I never understood, he kept his phone number unlisted.

These observations suggest that the members transferred attitudes into our group process that we had learned growing up, specifically: (1) Secrecy is important; (2) lying can be justified; (3) hostility is not acceptable; and (4) adoptees should not be trusted. No one wrote these attitudes into the charter of our organization. No one embraced them as ideals. They probably gained expression only outside conscious intent. Still, these attitudes existed. People repeat what they fail to remember. We did not remember clearly the oppressive aspects of our adoptive pasts.

Nevertheless, I felt an initial excitement upon joining a search group. Part of the excitement came from finally having the opportunity to talk about my adoption. Part of it reflected the hope that I might for the first time in my life really belong to something. My experience did not lead me to feel like a completely legitimate (the word suggests itself) member of anything. I could partially belong to many groups, but completely to none. Maybe ALMA would be different. After all, my birthright made me a legitimate member of a group of illegitimates. It should have been perfect. Who among us could have cast the first stone?

The excitement did not last, and the situation fell short of perfect. After a year or so, my experience in ALMA became like that of all the other organizations of my life. The group members and I had many things in common, but that did not automatically confer a sense of belonging. Perhaps I would finally experience a sense of belonging upon meeting my birthfamily. But perhaps not. I was beginning to have my doubts.

During the first few years of my ALMA membership, I became involved with several group members. If I could not find my birthmother and a group birthmother could not find her son, at least we could find each other. These relationships entailed a form of searching. They also involved acting out. Connections, of course, existed between the two. In general, benefits accrue to those who stay open to experience, especially if they can simultaneously remain curious about the experience. We remember by repeating, as well as by recalling. We learn by watching actions, as well as by listening to words. I often felt we learned more in our group about the adoptive experience when we were not overtly talking about adoption. Our actions below the table related to what we said above the table, and frequently our behavior provided more information than our words.

Several factors set me apart from the group. For one, not everybody entertains theoretical speculations like those mentioned above. The few psychologically-minded members of the group embraced theoretical perspectives other than psychodynamic and had little understanding of the concepts I espoused. Also, I ended up as the only member who did not find his birth-family and therefore could not participate in the show-and-tell activities that accompanied finding first families. Finally, I distrusted the purported salutary psychological benefits of search and reunion. Other members did not. I viewed my beliefs as theoretically sound, whereas others saw them as sour grapes.

I hoped to find search assistance in ALMA, but also wanted to find experience. The experience part made the group important early in my search. Just as memories sometimes express themselves as behavior rather than thoughts, so did many of my early search efforts express themselves as behavior rather than thinking. Although I wrote letters and asked questions in an effort to find my family, I also, via feelings transferred to group members, hoped to experience my family. The experience part did not work so well, but it did provide useful insights.

My relationship with Karen illustrates this point. I shared views on adoption more with Karen than with any other group member. Also, she was young and pretty and therefore easy to idealize. Karen planned to spend the summer sailing around New Zealand with a friend. I asked her if she would miss me during her trip. She was not sure she would miss me but felt certain that someone, somewhere, did (my birthmother). If one is looking for perfect in psychoanalysis, it doesn't get any better than this. Karen did not give me what I wanted (her), but she did tell me something important about myself (that I viewed her as my birthmother). And she did not charge me ninety dollars an hour for this insight.

My actual search began with a call to my adoptive father. Talking to one's adoptive parents provides the best way to begin a search because adoptive parents have the most information. It took me several months to develop the courage to call my father, and even then I could only muster an indirect question: I asked why they waited fourteen years to adopt me. He answered that they must have been so happy to have me they just didn't think of it. Fourteen years of giddy delirium! Where had I been during all the fun? Father's response disappointed and insulted me. In view of his obvious resistance, I saw little purpose in continuing our conversation. I simply got angry and resolved to proceed without his assistance. Maybe a kinder, gentler person could have handled the situation with more delicacy and obtained more information. But I could not. Some female adoptees in our group felt they could obtain information from Stanley if he were their father. Perhaps they could— women probably act with more tact and finesse than men do. Also, female adoptees carry more clout with their adoptive parents, since adoptive parents prefer them two to one.

My search has been accompanied every step of the way by the demeaning aspect that I remain almost entirely subject to the personal biases of individuals who are in a position to provide important information. It is my mother, my father, my name, my family, my heritage, and my choice that these people matter to me, but someone else always determines whether I learn of them. Sometimes these people help, sometimes they do not; but never do I have a "right" to the information. Even the State of Wisconsin, which enacted a law requiring the Division of Social Services to conduct a search for all adoptees who ask, has determined I do not qualify for this assistance; they say I cannot prove my birth occurred in Wisconsin. With respect to the issues of my adoption, I travel through our society in the back of the bus—and I bitterly resent it.

If my father intended to give me inane answers, I intended to talk to other relatives. I started with my favorites. With few exceptions, these relatives understood and supported my interest in the adoption. But they offered little help. Having been a black-market placement, with my position in the family unofficial, if not illegal, my adoptive parents had said as little as possible about the adoption. My relatives told me they had no information, and for the most part, I believed them.

I next wrote the State of California, attempting to obtain my original birth certificate. The birth certificate I possess is a joke—a California court-ordered, delayed certificate of birth listing the Andersens as my parents; Chicago as my birthplace; and April 16, 1940, as my birth date. The certificate is incorrect as to person, place, and time. If it was a living document, someone would commit it. California informed me they had no useful information (the story of my search) and stated that Illinois could never locate my original birth certificate (surprise).

I became angry. I had not expected my father to be helpful, but I anticipated completing my search without him. Now it appeared that I had been more deliberately separated from my past than I imagined. My roots had not been merely pulled out and replanted; they had been systematically severed in a bonsai-your-baby program intended to make children like me more marketable. I immediately phoned my father and demanded some answers. I wanted to know what kind of place I came from that no one registered my birth. I may have been unwanted, but damn it, even unwanted children are assigned numbers and listed in a ledger somewhere; there are laws about these things. Reacting to my indignation and because he heard I had been talking to my relatives, Father decided to "confess" the black-market nature of my placement.

Reluctantly, he told me I was born in Milwaukee and that they obtained me through the black market. He had never seen an original birth certificate. My birth occurred in a residential house, not a hospital or a boarding home. Stanley could not remember the name or address of the woman who ran the house. He never met my birthmother, knew nothing about my natural parents, paid $250 for me, and heard about the home through Ralph Jansen at the Danish Brotherhood. The black-market component obviously bothered him. He cried while telling me about it, talked about how he and Ann had led honorable lives, and claimed that buying a baby constituted their major misdeed. He had regretted that act all his life. Stanley revealed his feelings about the black-market aspect more readily than he provided facts about my natural family. I had to interrupt him and ask specific questions to get the above information.

Learning of Milwaukee as my birthplace amazed me, not so much because of geography, but because important information existed that remained so difficult for me to obtain and so easy for someone else to reveal. But this new information, while shocking and important, did not advance my search. I could advertise in the *Milwaukee Journal* instead of the *Chicago Tribune,* but still did not have a name, address, or even a birth date and now had reason to believe that no one ever registered my birth.

My father never told me anything more about my adoption although I did everything possible to convince him to do so. He reacted badly to any mention of the adoption. Stanley said he and Ann had always thought well of me, but now this interest in my natural family tarnished his memories. He wished he had died with my mother so he could have avoided witnessing this ungrateful dereliction of responsibility (my words). He also stated that he better not ever learn I intended to meet my "real mother," implying he would disown me. (Adoptees apparently come with interminable cancellation policies, policies that adoptive parents redeem in fifteen percent of adoptions.) Somewhere in our conversations I asked my father what would have happened to me if he and Ann had died before the court hearing. He imagined that I would have gone "back" to an orphanage. For one thing, I did not come "from" an orphanage (although an orphanage might have outclassed my maternity home). For another, Stanley never would have imagined that a natural son of his in such a situation would ever have ended up in an orphanage.

I next advertised in the *Milwaukee Journal.* Doing so proved no simple task. One could probably advertise more easily in the classified section for underwater group-sex partners than declare an interest in finding your biological parents—perhaps because giving up one's children offends society more than underwater group-sex does. The newspaper people ask a number of questions, refer you to various supervisors, and ultimately submit the advertisement to an executive who can authorize publication. This ordeal probably reflects the litigious nature of our society more than it makes a statement about adoption, but this complicated procedure does not make an already difficult situation any less strained. Whoring around trying to meet your parents is a tacky experience, although with time and practice it does become easier.

I have had no success running advertisements, but continue to do so. Every Christmas the *Milwaukee Journal* prints a cheery little notice that I still want to meet my birthparents. Every Christmas no one calls. When I first started advertising, a few search assistants responded. These assistants proved helpful because they put me in contact with people in Wisconsin who have assisted with some necessary, if not especially productive, search work.

As a result of one of these contacts, I talked with Meg Kissinger, a reporter from the *Journal,* who expressed an interest in doing an adoption story. Six years ago in a Sunday edition, Meg Kissinger wrote a lengthy article about my search experience. Better than a classified advertisement because of its visibility, the story chronicled my history and ended with my phone number in St. Louis. I hoped this article would help my search. Also, I realized that spreading the story of my black-market placement all over the Sunday edition of Milwaukee's major newspaper was not something my adoptive parents would have appreciated. Yet I experienced a certain poetic justice in turning such a tightly guarded secret into public record. Some would call that progress. Others would not.

Although having the article published helped me psychologically, it proved of no practical value to my search—no calls resulted. Consistently in my search, promising leads have fizzled out. Responding to an ad, a woman once called and claimed to be my mother; she was not. ALMA thought they matched me with a sister; they did not. An audio-cassette from an uncle, the one most likely to know something about my adoption, turned out to be twenty minutes of nothing. The Wisconsin search coordinator told me after checking the illegitimate birth certificates that I might have correctly identified my birthplace and date; I apparently did not. Evelyn Jansen authoritatively told me I had been shipped to Milwaukee from Kentucky or Tennessee—not true. I could go on and on with similar examples. The disappointments of my search have tempered my expectations. My birthmother might just call one day and I could end up telling her she has the wrong number.

A member of my search group told me she read in *Reader's Digest* that most black-market babies came from prostitutes. None of the adoptees in our group had prostitutes for birthmothers, but none of these people came through the black market. Their histories all included agencies, records, case workers, and birth certificates—the kind of things that make for legal placements and successful searches. I do not know if many black-market babies ever came from prostitutes, but the idea made sense. Even if only a small percentage of black-market babies came from hookers, my mother may have been one of them. For those of you who have never had to consider whether your mother walked the streets, let me tell you that the issue assumes some importance.

Given a choice, most people would prefer their mother be a teacher, secretary, or nurse (or an astronaut, neurosurgeon, or helicopter pilot), rather than a prostitute. The world's oldest profession may be long on tradition, but it is short on prestige. Knowing I came through the black market altered the probabilities of my heritage. While the medical profession has no immunity against producing illegitimate children, doctors and nurses typically do not sell their children. Prostitutes sometimes do. One can easily find stories about drug addicts who sell their bodies and babies to pay for their habits. I did not enjoy considering that my mother may have sold herself, although facing an unpleasant truth beats embracing a pleasant lie.

The whole dark side seemed unreal. My subjective history included such things as Boy Scouts, baseball, and paid tax receipts. Now it appeared necessary to incorporate issues like prostitution and selling children if I wanted a comprehensive picture of my history. Issues such as this do not easily integrate. I may not have been born to a hooker, but the possibility existed, and whether most or only a few black-market babies came from prostitutes did not obviate the need to consider this as a potential part of my identity.

Does it matter if one's birthmother was a harlot instead of a nurse? I think so. Would you rather have a race horse out of Winning Colors (the filly who won the 1987 Kentucky Derby) or the mare down the road? What do people mean by the phrases: Blood is thicker than water; chip off the old block; like father, like son; it's in the blood? What is meant by the proverb, "The daughter of a crab does not give birth to a bird"? Why do so many singers have children who can sing, athletes have children who are athletic, professors have children who are bright, and alcoholics have children who drink too much? How comfortable would you be with your daughter dating the adoptive boy down the street if the boy's biological father and grand-father were both in prison for murder?

Our genes largely determine our biology, psychology, and characters. Although environment plays a role in human development, it merely interacts with biology; it does not eradicate it. I did not like the implications associated with trying on the identity of a prostitute's son, although my concerns were more general than specific—my mind does not readily grasp the concept of a male prostitute. Did I now have to worry about my moral and ethical judgments? What did this say about who could have been my father? Did this mean the maternity home concocted the doctor-nurse business just to boost sales?

I thought about my experience with the two prostitutes (call girls) I had known professionally. (They employed me.) Actually, they were interesting people—attractive, assertive women who paid their bills (in cash) and who were anything but dull. In addition, one of them maintained a "social" relationship with a former American League MVP and also provided services to several other famous professional athletes. The other lady had apparently been called to work one night when a Supreme Court Justice came to town. I found this interesting, but continued to grumble about my heredity until a friend decided that a call girl and an MVP sounded more exciting than a doctor and a nurse. (Actually, by this time a question arose about whether my birthfather had been a dentist rather than a physician, and my birthmother a dental assistant rather than a nurse—various relatives remembering different stories.) Maybe my friend called it right. Perhaps a Supreme Court Justice and a call girl has more pizazz than a dentist and a dental assistant. Why not? Think positive! I would not mind having a father who won the American League MVP award.

An interesting idea began to emerge. I had been hanging my head about the possibility my mother had been a hooker, but why not consider the advantages? Perhaps I might do well in barroom fights. Possibly I come from a line of survivors. Maybe my mother was pretty. Maybe my genes help me to be pragmatic, businesslike, or unconventional. Driving home one evening, I played with this idea and came up with a brief satire. This "work" took the form of a specialty catalogue for adoptees. Most, but not all, of my adoptee and birthmother friends found it amusing. A sample of the items from this catalogue includes:

> **Bedtime Favorites**: Get this collector's edition of these all-time favorite adoptee stories. Includes the beautiful *Chosen Child* and *My Mother Loved Me So Much She Gave Me Up.* Also contains the dramatic *Your Birthparents Crashed and Burned,* as well as the suspense thriller *Be Good or We'll Take You Back.* These and many other stories you can read again and again in this beautifully bound volume.
>
> $39.95

> **Silver Jewelry:** Affirm your position as an adoptee with the metal long known for being second best. Silver jewelry cast as street urchins, puppy dogs, and nondescript globs void of historical significance.
>
> $24.75

> **The Illegitimate's Guide to Unwed Mothers' Homes:** The most comprehensive guide on the market. Over 1,200 listings with addresses, descriptions, and photographs. Turn that routine vacation into a nostalgic adventure with a visit to the very place where your mother signed you away.
>
> $19.95

While I could find some humor in my search and think more positively about my birthmother, the search itself produced little. While others in my search group found parents, I had to console myself by writing articles and satires. I would have preferred having lunch with my birthmother to creating more adoptee products, but I did not have that choice. Like everyone else, I became more active in my search efforts when I had a good lead. My good leads, however, were running out. Additional avenues always exist, but one can only spend so much time and energy pursuing them. A person could, for example, perhaps mortgage his house and take out a full-page ad in the *New York Times.* But no one ever does. Search always involves relative values.

Chapter Ten

It isn't whether you win or lose, it's how you play the game

For my part, I travel not to go anywhere, but to go. I travel for travel's sake. The great affair is to move.
—*Robert Louis Stevenson*

I had now searched three or four years and learned little more than that I was born in Milwaukee. I did not search every day. No one does that. Typically, one makes a flurry of activity, then follows it with a latent period when he or she emotionally digests the experience and also adjusts to the disappointment if the efforts proved unsuccessful. By this time I had talked to all my relatives. I had done everything possible to elicit information from my adoptive father, whose refusal to help became an incapacity to help as Alzheimer's disease erased his memory. My adoption decree provided no assistance. The State of

California had no useful information. There was no original birth certificate. The lawyer who handled my adoption could not or would not help. Newspaper advertisements produced nothing. And an excellent search assistant did some fancy things with the Milwaukee and Madison birth records, allowing her to identify many of the illegitimate births in Milwaukee on or about my birth date, but this work proved of no practical value.

I was no closer to a name, address, or telephone number than ever. If the point of searching is to find, then my search had been a complete bust. Some people say philosophy is for losers, perhaps because only the losers have time to consider how the game is played—winners being preoccupied celebrating their victories. I had to hope search entailed more than finding. Perhaps, after all, the philosophers have it right and it does matter how the game is played.

Changes began to occur in my posture *vis-à-vis* the search. I became less timid about writing letters and asking questions. The search group assumed less importance, in part because I learned to recognize my transference reactions, but also because our group tended to avoid the emotional issues of adoption and I had exhausted their search tips. Finally, I adjusted to the possibility that my mother had been a prostitute. I even liked the idea. If one's life must be tacky, it might as well be tacky with flair.

My father had told me he learned of my maternity home through Ralph Jansen at the Danish Brotherhood. Ralph and Evelyn Jansen socialized with my adoptive parents when we lived in Wisconsin. I tried to contact Ralph as soon as I learned of his role in my adoption, but he had died several months earlier. I did reach his son, who took offense when I tried to explain my reason for calling. I did not understand his reaction, although it may have been because both Ralph and Ralph Jr. were themselves adoptees. A negative response like this in the early years of my search upset me and diverted me to other areas. Two years passed before I again tried to contact Evelyn.

By then I was a search veteran and more comfortable with my actions. I obtained her address and wrote for information.

Three weeks later she responded. Evelyn, rather than Ralph, had in fact told the Andersens about my maternity home. She responded in a straightforward manner, which was both unusual and refreshing, and indicated I had been a black-market baby born in either Kentucky or Tennessee. I quickly called to confirm this surprising information. Evelyn restated her conviction about my birthplace and felt certain my father knew this as well.

Her new information dramatically affected my search, if not my life, although it appears today that the information was incorrect. It all but ended my relationship with my adoptive father. I had made my interest in the adoption perfectly clear, and in view of this new material, even Stanley's black-market confession appeared to have been dishonest. Self-respect would not allow me to continue a relationship in which the rules exclusively favored my father.

Because Stanley and I experienced technical difficulties with our telephone conversations, I asked an uncle to talk with him about the Kentucky-Tennessee business. Uncle Les delayed speaking to him because Stanley was suffering from an acute respiratory infection, in addition to his Alzheimer and Parkinson's diseases. I could understand waiting to bring up this matter, but had become weary of having this issue deferred because one or the other of my adoptive parents supposedly could not handle it. I am uncertain whether Lester ever did talk to my father, but I certainly had reached the limit of my tolerance for the lies, stonewalling, and deceit about my adoption. I never talked to my adoptive father again. Stanley Andersen died of pneumonia two years later, at age seventy-four. Most adoptive parents probably do not envision the relationship with their child ending as mine did with my adoptive father. A lesson can be learned here: Adoptive parents should pick their child from better stock than did Stanley and

Ann Andersen, or they should tell that child the truth about his or her past.

Evelyn Jansen's information about my birthplace sent me on a chase through the land of racehorses and country music. I spoke with authorities in Lexington and Nashville, ordered hats, sweatshirts, and football jerseys from the Universities of Kentucky and Tennessee, worshipped everyone's Southern accents, and fell in love with every woman in this region whom I talked with on the telephone. I learned that during the depression young girls from the

Stanley Andersen (1913-1988).

hills of these states surrendered their children in record numbers. I forgot Milwaukee, became homesick watching television events from these states, advertised in the area's newspapers, and pestered my friends with this new information. My secretary gave me a white-trash cookbook, and I became more comfortable with my lack of tidiness, as I imagined that my birthmother's front yard was once littered with chickens, bicycles, and automobile parts. I learned of the Tennessee Children's Home.

The Tennessee Children's Home ran perhaps this country's largest black-market baby operation. In the 1930s and 1940s this home placed over five thousand children in all regions of the United States. They became a national, if not international, corporation. The home attracted birthmothers from Tennessee,

Arkansas, Missouri, Illinois, Kentucky, Mississippi, Louisiana, and West Virginia. The Tennessee Children's Home was an ethical black hole, but a profitable business. Tennessee finally closed it down in 1954, but never pursued criminal prosecution because the major operator died of cancer three months after the state's action. The abundant supply of babies, the home's unscrupulous methods, and the corrupt cooperation of a judge who could supply official, if not legal, adoption decrees provided the elements for the financial success of this home. The Tennessee Children's Home earned four dollars for legally placing a child in Shelby County, whereas it collected two hundred to one thousand dollars for selling a child out of state—a nice profit margin, a big business.

Home at last! Apparently I had at least located my statistically probable place of birth. I am one of the few people whose birthplace changes from year to year. For one percent of my life I considered it to be Lexington; for three percent, Memphis; for eighty-six percent, Chicago; and for ten percent, Milwaukee. Perhaps I should keep a running count and at a point merely declare one of these cities official.

The state archived the records from the Tennessee Children's Home and moved them to Nashville. I wrote to the Division of Social Services and requested information about these records, telling them I had possibly once resided in this home and indicating there would be no record of my adoption. Hopefully, they could look at the records of children born around my birth date and see if any of them fit my description. Nashville responded that they had no record of anyone named Andersen adopting a child from the Tennessee Children's Home. That should have been no surprise—I gave them that information. Upon clarification, I learned that the files were indexed by adoptive and natural names. They were not indexed by date. My name might be there, but it could be anywhere among five thousand records, most or all of them sealed by court order.

By coincidence, I had been conversing with a Memphis lawyer. We discussed my situation and considered what might be done to access these records. He intended to explore the situation, but we pursued this matter no further. If I knew my name was definitely in these records, the issue of cost would become unimportant. But we were discussing the possibility of hiring a lawyer to petition a judge to allow someone access to five thousand sealed adoption records. Such a motion would require a lot of work, and the chances for success would be minimal. The only certainty would be the legal fees. Breaking and entering would probably be more cost effective.

A more reasonable approach was to follow Evelyn Jansen's lead about another woman who obtained a child from my maternity home. Evelyn could only remember the woman's maiden name, Erma Vontard, which made tracking her down rather difficult. Checking the telephone directories produced no Vontards in Racine or Milwaukee. I wrote my aunt in Racine, who recalled a Vontard Construction Company in Racine some time in the 1960s and remembered that the company had been sold to the Superior Construction Company. A call to Superior revealed that Paul Vontard had owned the Vontard Construction Company and he had died fifteen years earlier. Paul Vontard left no children.

Feeling I had reached the limits of my investigative abilities, I hired a detective. O'Brien Investigations sounded official, so I secured the services of Sergeant Terrence O'Brien. Twenty-five hundred dollars later, Sergeant O'Brien gave me the following information: Erma Vontard married Karl Adolph Sorenson. They adopted a daughter, Karen, born on December 29, 1939. Both Karen and her father lived in Stevens Point, Wisconsin. Erma had died several years earlier. John and Marie Hansen had also obtained a child from this home. The Hansens, both still alive, lived in Racine. Their daughter, Elizabeth, resided in Milwaukee.

Terry and I both talked to Karl Sorenson. Although he was friendly and cooperative, Karl remembered little about the adoption. He thought the maternity home had been in the southern part of Milwaukee, but could not remember the address. He could not remember the name of the woman who ran the home or tell us anything about her. He said getting a child from this home was like "picking up a sack of potatoes." Karl told us about John and Marie Hansen. Karl seemed fairly candid, but when I asked why he waited fifteen years to adopt his daughter, he indicated they must have done things in that way back then. I think not.

John and Marie Hansen differed markedly from Karl Sorenson. While they retained their memories, these people had no desire to help. They were disturbed that anyone would want to inquire about their daughter, especially after so many years. Unlike my parents and the Sorensons, John and Marie never adopted their daughter. Instead, they obtained a false birth certificate naming themselves as the natural parents. They then raised this child as if she had been born to them. Marie had lost a premature baby in 1934. She then lost a full-term girl in 1936. She wrote to me, "It was three years later, almost to the very same date, that John and I took the North Shore train to Milwaukee and brought home our baby, Elizabeth, named the same as the darling we had lost three years earlier. We felt as if God had given our baby back to us!" Apparently John and Marie did not fully grieve the loss of their first two children.

The Hansens discovered Jesus soon after obtaining Elizabeth. Their letters came packed with Pentecostal religious material, all proclaiming the inconsequence of earthly concerns (i.e., adoption?) compared to everlasting salvation. John and Marie's religious fervor caused major difficulties in the relationship with their daughter, as no doubt did their emotional confusion about which Elizabeth they were raising. The Hansens felt that God returned their deceased daughter to them in the person of Elizabeth, a belief which apparently contributed to their religious conversion.

Evidence indicated that no one ever told Elizabeth about her adoption, and I did not wish to be the first to provide her this information. John and Marie insisted I not contact her. They also appeared to lie about their adoption in the same self-righteous manner my father always lied to me about mine. My tolerance for lies at this point approached zero. I became angry and wanted to take the issue directly to Elizabeth, but worried how she would react if she had not yet learned of her adoption. A major concern in my life had been that expressing an interest in my past might threaten the well-being of my adoptive mother, and I could easily transfer that dynamic into this situation and envision Elizabeth jumping off a bridge as a result of my introducing this information. As a compromise, I thought that threatening to tell the Hansen's daughter might be a way to force more information from John and Marie. But I wondered about this tactic and questioned my direction. The most unlaw ful thing I had ever done was break into my high school gymnasium to practice basketball. Now I found myself plotting blackmail and extortion. I was becoming either assertive or corrupt. I considered it assertive.

Writing to the Hansens, I expressed my reluctance to contact Elizabeth but also stressed my interest in learning about my heritage. My letter included a comprehensive list of questions; this was legal, perhaps, but probably still constituted extortion. They responded by pleading forgetfulness. I could have continued to press the issue, but did not enjoy badgering these septuagenarians and could see no purpose in further upsetting them. On the other hand, Elizabeth possibly possessed invaluable information and I had few other leads. Considerable, but circumstantial, evidence suggested that Elizabeth did not know about her adoption, whereas the Hansens indicated they had told her. Based on their statement, which could have been a lie, I sent Elizabeth a letter.

Several weeks later she responded. She had, in fact, learned of her adoption at the time of her marriage. One of her children did not yet know about the adoption, and she worried what this knowledge might do to his relationship with his grandparents. She spoke freely about her past difficulties with her parents and told me she married at eighteen to get out of the house. For the past thirty-two years her parents never mentioned the adoption, and I upset them with my contact and questions. Elizabeth always wanted to find her birthfamily, but never attempted to do so. She urged me not to contact her parents, since the whole thing distressed them and she worried about their health. (Adoptees always worry about their adoptive parents health.) Elizabeth intended to obtain more information, but she could not determine how to proceed. We talked several times, our conversations being pleasant and informative.

Perhaps the Hansens could today provide information that would help locate my maternity home. Elizabeth most likely will never approach them. I probably won't either. I felt no guilt about upsetting the Hansens, but thought I should go no further with them. For reasons that remain unclear, the issue became a question of personal integrity, and it made little sense to compromise the very thing that through search I hoped to attain.

Several months later Marie and John sent me another letter. They wanted to show me some advice from *Dr. James Dobson's Focus on the Family Bulletin* on how to rear well-adjusted adoptive children. Doctor Dobson advised:

> . . . Tell him he was specially <u>chosen</u>. This way the child will be comfortable with the idea of adoption. When he asks about his biological parents, respond in a matter-of-fact manner. You can suggest inoffensive, vague possibilities why his natural parents offered him for adoption. . . . Give him details about that first day and how the Lord answered your prayers. Don't be

> afraid of using the word <u>adopted</u> openly. After you
> and your child have discussed his adoption and he has
> accepted the idea over a period of time, however, there
> is no reason to continue to bring up the subject. Let it
> fade naturally as melding into the family takes place.

I disagree with Dr. Dobson. The adoption issues might fade, but
they hardly do so naturally, and Dr. Dobson's indifference to
honesty will not facilitate the process.

I talked with Karen Sorenson, the other person we knew
to have been placed through my maternity home. Karen had
never wished to search, although both her father and daughter
encouraged her to do so. Karen refrained from searching because she believed (erroneously) that only adoptees from problematic homes looked for their birthparents and she had experienced no problems with her adoptive family. Wisconsin has
enacted a state law allowing adoptees to receive nonidentifying
information about their birthfamilies. Wisconsin also requires the
state to do a search at the adoptee's request. I asked Karen if she
would write for her nonidentifying information. Her place of
birth and the name of the person signing her birth certificate
interested me, and if Karen did not want this information for
herself, perhaps she could simply forward the unopened corres-
pondence to me. She would never have to look at it. Karen
expressed an interest in the material. I talked with her several
times about this matter, and several times she assured me she
would write. But she hasn't, and she won't. Karen apparently
holds views on adoption that she does not share with me.

Mary Emery, the search assistant who did the work for
me with the Milwaukee and Madison birth records, did additional things as well, including a review of all the known
maternity homes in Milwaukee at the time of my birth. One of
these homes looked promising, and with each additional piece of
information we tried to assess the possibility of this facility being
my birthplace. A midwife, who was also a licensed practical

nurse, ran the home. It was a wood-frame, two-story house in a residential neighborhood—fitting the description given by all the adoptive parents. Also, being only two blocks from a train station, the Hansens could easily have arrived there on the North Shore train. The home sat in the southern part of the greater Milwaukee area in a community called West Allis.

According to neighbors, the proprietor appeared to be someone capable of conducting a shady business. Also, she maintained a close relationship with a physician, and he could have provided her with official, yet inaccurate, birth certificates. We talked to many people about this home. A neighbor remembered that about one woman a month would stay there. They appeared to be "presentable" women, who always arrived and departed in automobiles, but otherwise kept out of sight. While most people at this time did not own automobiles, Theresa Kusiak, the proprietor of this establishment, owned a Ford Victoria ("the best car on the block"), which she lost when her maternity home closed. Finally, while about twelve deliveries a year occurred here, we found no birth certificates listing this address as the place of birth.

I enjoyed hearing about this establishment. Mary took a photograph of the house and also obtained one of Ms. Kusiak, but none of this material proved familiar to any of the adoptive parents. Theresa Kusiak died in 1958. She had no children. All her belongings went to her nephew, who recalls that he threw away the home's records shortly after his aunt's death. Interestingly, he used the term "receipts" rather than records when referring to the material from the maternity home. We have learned nothing more about Theresa Kusiak's maternity business.

I next attempted to avail myself of the services offered by the State of Wisconsin. Writing to them about my situation, I indicated what would facilitate my search. The most useful information would be the illegitimate boys (who had never been adopted) born in Milwaukee on or about April 13, 1940. The state has this information, and not many people would fit that description. The state also could determine if Karen Sorenson had an original birth certificate, and if so, they could compare her place of birth with that of the illegitimate boys born on about my date of birth. Simple, huh? My birth certificate, if I had one, would never have been sealed. I could simply ask for and receive it, without breaking any laws.

Theresa Kusiak's maternity home: 1103 S. 86th Street—two blocks from the State Fair Grounds.

I talked at length several times with Carol Swanson, the woman who heads the office responsible for performing Wisconsin searches. She thought I might be correct about my birthplace, but would never tell me why. Throughout our entire contact Ms. Swanson never dropped her officious and condescending attitude, and she told me that adoptees gained little from finding their birthfamilies. She mainly attempted to determine whether Wisconsin had any responsibility for me, since my birth certificate said I was born in Illinois. We never got beyond that point. It took her four months to conclude that Wisconsin would do nothing because I could not prove Wisconsin as my birthplace. The woman said it was too bad my parents had lied about my birthplace; she felt it showed a lack of foresight on their part.

Adoptees may be meek and unassuming, but this was too much. I was furious. While I rarely complain, this situation proved the exception. I wrote a letter to the Secretary of the Department of Social Services and one to the Governor. These letters were not intended to change the state's position *vis-à-vis* my search, but rather, to express my feeling that Ms. Swanson should be excluded from adoptee issues. I didn't care what Wisconsin did with their records. How well I played the game mattered more to me at this time than winning or losing my search, and playing well at this point meant reacting to this outrage. My motivation was intrinsic. I expected no action to result from these letters. None did. The state officials did respond. The Governor seemed to express genuine concern; the Secretary did not.

I sent a copy of these letters to my search assistant in Wisconsin. The letters had the unintended side effect of helping to crystalize a class-action suit by the Wisconsin search people to remove Carol Swanson from her position. My reaction to Ms. Swanson had been typical. Wisconsin adoptees and birthparents consider her a hindrance more than a help. Carol Swanson spends part of her time warning Wisconsin hospitals to watch for people asking for birth records, lest they thereby locate their natural families. Search is difficult enough without having to contend with people of this ilk. Perhaps Ms. Swanson's aptitudes would be more fully realized if she worked in law enforcement rather than human services.

I remain guarded that additional search leads will prove successful. Too many promising leads have miscarried, and picking oneself up after each disappointment becomes tiresome. Most recently, we tried to learn something about Leland Trump, the physician who falsified the birth certificate on Elizabeth Hansen. My birthfather allegedly was a physician. In Doctor Trump we had both a physician as well as someone connected to my maternity home. While Doctor Trump probably was not my birthfather, he became a more likely candidate than any other human being on the planet. I wrote the medical society to see if they had any information on him. Surprisingly, they did. Leland Trump proved to be a colorful character.

Doctor Trump allegedly obtained his medical degree from Marquette University in 1916. He was fifty-five years old at the time of my birth. Doctor Trump was no Marcus Welby. Five years out of medical school, he was charged him with auto theft, having paid Joseph Carr, a roadhouse waiter, seven hundred dollars to steal him a "large touring car." Subsequently, Doctor Trump apparently built a thriving medical practice as an abortionist, for which authorities arrested him in 1932. At the time of his arrest, six women were present in his clinic, three having received his services and three awaiting them. He charged two hundred dollars for an abortion. In the middle of the great depression, $1200 a day was an incredible amount of money.

Leland Trump married twice. For reasons which Mary and I could never understand, he misrepresented the date of his first marriage when he applied for his second marriage license. He also apparently lied about his date of graduation from Marquette Medical School. We thought it would be a worthwhile endeavor to get a picture of this man, which we expected to do via his medical class photograph. We obtained the class photograph, but Leland Trump was not in it, and no record indicated he had ever attended Marquette. Doctor Trump had one son, but this son died at the age of twenty-eight. There was no photograph, no children, no close relatives, and an apparent string of lies. What should have been an easy task, obtaining Leland Trump's photograph, turned into a major project. My enthusiasm for searching wanes when the odds are so long and everything so difficult.

I have learned little as a result of my search efforts. Today, I again consider Milwaukee my birthplace and assume my birth date to be April 13, 1940. These assumptions put me about where I was at the start of my search. I recently talked with the president of the American Adoption Congress, who is an acknowledged expert on handling difficult searches. She felt confident she could help. A problem developed concerning the approach we discussed, but I will certainly try to avail myself of any assistance she might offer.

At times I become indifferent to finding my birthfamily. Having been especially busy in recent months, I remember thinking that if my birthmother called I probably would take her number and call her back at my convenience. At other times I acutely experience my disconnection and very much wish to complete my search. Not long ago I attended an adoption meeting in Chicago, a city closely tied to my years in Wisconsin. Meetings such as this provide support, empathy, and under-standing, as well as stir up feelings about one's adoption experi-ence. They also end too quickly. As I drove off by myself in the rain following this meeting, leaving behind my friends and my fantasized expectations, the freeway signs pointed the route north to Milwaukee. Milwaukee is no longer just another city to me. Milwaukee was, and will always be, where I should have belonged. It is the place of my roots, the place of my family, the place of my dreams. I have never lived there, but I have never left there. I should have been heading north to Milwaukee, but was, as always, heading south to somewhere else. Heading south I would drive out of the rain, but not out of my tears.

My search still has options. I can contact various search experts, push harder to find out about Karen Sorenson's birth certificate, and advertise in the Milwaukee newspapers. I could contact people delivered by Doctor Trump or Theresa Kusiak, as well as people born at other addresses that might provide leads. And I could again contact the Hansens. Also, my birthmother might some day read this book and contact me.

I continue to search and will do so for as long as I am able. I search in order to one day contact my natural family. I search, also, because in some ways searching matters as much as finding.

Chapter Eleven

Search and consequences

One ship drives east and another drives west
With the selfsame winds that blow.
'Tis the set of sails and not the gales
Which tells us the way to go.
                    —*Rose Hartwick Thorpe*

Although my search has not proven successful when measured by usual standards, important consequences have transpired. Changes have occurred in my life as a result of dealing with my adoption. Dealing with adoption and searching are not synonymous, but the overlap is so great it becomes hard to consider one without the other.

Searching for birthparents used to be viewed as a manifestation of psychopathology—people thought only disturbed adoptees looked for their natural families. But this has not proven true, and recently a number of authorities have viewed search as a useful way to cope with the problems of being an adoptee.

I published an article several years ago suggesting two models of searching as therapeutic. The most prevalent of these I called the medical or deficiency model. In this model one views the adoptee as suffering from something akin to a deficiency disease. The deficiency is considered to be either a lack of information (i.e., not knowing why the birthmother gave one away), or a lack of experience (i.e., the narcissistic investment of the birthmother). Through search and reunion the adoptee can obtain the missing information or experience and thereby become whole. The goal is cure. Treatment is complete. The curative agent remains external to the adoptee. Finding is imperative for the treatment to occur.

The other model is the psychological or trauma model. In this model one views adoption as a post-traumatic stress disorder. Treatment consists of acknowledging and responding to the trauma and attempting to change the experience from one that was passively endured to one that is actively mastered. The goal in this model is growth rather than cure. Treatment remains incomplete. The therapeutic agent is internal. Finding is not imperative for improvement to occur.

Not surprisingly, I embrace the psychological model. Why would I want to believe that the key to my health and happiness resides with a birthmother I cannot find? Doing so would only make me miserable. Certainly the status of my search influences my views regarding searching, but it does not invalidate these views. Everyone involved in adoption has biases. If we discounted their ideas, we would be left with nothing except opinions from people indifferent to the subject—that would hardly be progress. We need to appreciate our biases and to consider them in our formulations, but it is neither possible nor desirable to eliminate them. Further, one should note that I formulated my viewpoint long before I encountered my search problems. In addition, I have undergone salutary changes even without finding my birthfamily. Finally, many reunions appear to produce little therapeutic effect.

Even I have reasons to embrace the medical model. While I may not be able to locate the key to health and happiness, this model at least offers the promise that such a key exists; cure, identity, and self-completion are just waiting to be discovered. The psychological model makes no such promises. It offers more modest goals and demands a higher price. Given a choice, who would find the psychological model message appealing? Also, the medical model entices with its simplicity; potential happiness merely requires that one seek and find.

I have taken liberty to overstate these two positions. The two views partially overlap, one can subscribe to both in varying degrees, and neither is entirely valid. Still, the psychological model approximates reality more closely, and people usually have a bias toward one view or the other.

Search may not be the only way to deal with being an adoptee, but it is the most obvious way. I would question how well an adoptee has resolved adoption issues if he actively refuses to search. Searching provides tangible things—people and places to which affects are associated. For example, at a recent meeting an adoptee told how she how she located her birthmother the very day after the woman had been buried. The birthmother had no other relatives. The adoptee paid a thousand dollars to exhume the body so she could see her mother's face and place a rose in the casket. No one viewed this as a casual experience. Many people cried upon hearing the story. Resolution in the psychological model occurs mainly through grief. People and places facilitate grieving. I cry more in Milwaukee than I do in New York. Almost any adoptee would be moved upon having his birthmother tell him that she cried every year on his birthday.

A midwest television personality helps place special-needs children for adoption. Being an adoptee himself, this newscaster no doubt gains something personally, as well as professionally, from the experience. Writing articles, getting involved politically, and helping others search represent common approaches people take in psychologically addressing their adoptions. Anything that actively confronts the issue provides benefit, with the possibilities limited only by one's creativity. Yet search generally remains central to such efforts, because it is so emotionally charged, and because it is there.

I would like to consider the consequences of my search, or to put it more accurately, the consequences of confronting my adoption. As stated earlier, I regard these changes as important, although most of them are intangible and difficult to describe. While on balance the changes are positive, they do not come free. Usually accompanying each gain, often tied to it by the logic of the situation, occurs a corresponding loss. The losses appear to be inevitable, but then rarely in life does one get something for nothing.

The positive consequences are: (1) I have more self-esteem. (2) I am not always infatuated. (3) I feel more authentic. (4) I have a better sense of identity. (5) My life has less pretense. (6) I can better assess possibilities. (7) I am not guilty about my interest in my birthfamily. (8) I am more aware of my reactions. (9) I am more comfortable with my judgements.

With the negatives these become: (1) I have more self-esteem, but cry all the time. (2) I avoid infatuation, but hardly fall in love at all. (3) I feel more authentic, but border on being eccentric. (4) I developed a stronger identity, but formed it out of thin air. (5) My life has less pretense, but I am more alone. (6) I assess possibilities better, but attempt fewer things. (7) I feel no guilt about my interest in my birthfamily, but my adoptive relationship collapsed. (8,9) I do not experience a problem with being more self-aware and confident in my judgment, but others might see me as less compromising.

In addition, I have changed jobs, moved to the country, surrounded myself with animals, invested in gold stocks, and become a vegetarian—all in part as a result of confronting my adoption. I am well on the way to becoming really me, not always considering this such a good idea, but certainly not wanting to turn back.

Self-esteem. My most obvious behavioral difference is that I now cry regularly, whereas before searching I cried infrequently. I cry about almost anything: my animals, music, sad stories, happy stories. I cry about my birthfamily, and not about my birthfamily. Seeing Bambi's mother get shot always made me cry, but now I cry watching such things as *China Beach, Life Goes On, Paradise, Tour of Duty,* etc., etc.—even *Night Court* and *Family Ties.* I cry not only about loss, but about any genuine expression of caring, admiration, or concern. Most often when crying I am not consciously thinking about my birthfamily. Frequently, my reasons for crying remain unclear.

Discussing this issue becomes difficult. Men are not supposed to cry—although society may be relaxing this prohibition a bit. Today men probably can cry at the loss of loved ones and at epoch moments in their lives without thereby compromising their identities. But they should not cry about the loss of material things, frustrated personal ambitions, or physical pain. I generally do not cry about those things, so in the contemporary view I apparently still get by.

Yet I do cry a lot. Getting into my adoption issues has exposed a loss, making me more sensitive because of its exposure. Thoughts of my adoption rarely leave my mind. They color everything. The images of the family I lost years ago reflect in my tears of today. And they will probably persist for a long time.

I have observed that along with the tears has come an increase in self-esteem. A connection probably exists. While other adoptees have made similar observations, support for the validity of this association remains largely anecdotal.

Such an association might be rooted in the logical consequences that follow from the adoptive family's assumption of the basic perspective from which to view the other triad members. This constitutes the "spin" they give the adoption experience, and it becomes a part of the adoptee's developmental milieu. If the adoptive family envisions the birthmother as a caring person, we get what might be called the "good people-bad situation" perspective. If the birthmother is viewed as uncaring, we get the "bad people-good situation" perspective. Since it is impossible, whether explicitly or implicitly, not to make such assumptions about the birthmother (birthfamily), adoptive families fall more or less into one of these two groups. Families prone to deny the pain of adoption generally choose the bad people-good situation perspective.

If one sees the birthmother as caring, it will be assumed she wanted to keep her child and that only forces beyond her control caused the disruption. One will envision the mother as thinking often of the child and as sad about this loss. The child also might be expected to think of his or her family and to wonder about the parents and siblings he or she will never know. This position sees no one as having wanted the disruption and envisions everyone as saddened by it. The problem becomes viewed as situational, rather than due to personalities. Crying constitutes the natural response to these circumstances—personal indictments do not.

From the other perspective one sees adoption as a wonderful option. The birthmother is viewed as having been able to get rid of an unwanted child, perhaps thereby freeing herself to pursue a career, a boyfriend, or whatever. She is not envisioned as regretting her decision and is assumed to have forgotten the child—just as the social workers promised her she would. Nothing remains to be sad about here since both the birthmother and child are thought to have "melded" into new lives and forgotten about each other.

The latter view obviates grief, but creates its own problems. The adoptee has to explain what made him so inconsequential that his mother could forget him, and he wonders why he could not fit into the life of this woman who left and lived happily ever after. Also, while adoption workers might say that surrendering a child for adoption constitutes an act of great love, society does not think highly of people who give away their kin. Most people view giving away one of their own as a major (although perhaps necessary) screw-up.

In another scenario from the bad people-good situation perspective, the birthmother can be envisioned as such a disaster that the adoptee is fortunate to have escaped living in the quagmire into which she certainly would have dragged them both. The adoption therefore becomes reason to rejoice rather than to grieve. This perspective also presents the adoptee a problem because it is difficult to avoid identifying with a person whose blood flows through your veins. If your mother was such a mess, what does that say about you? Again, the situation is good, but the people become suspect.

Given a choice between dealing with the adoption as good people in a flawed situation or flawed people in a good situation, I would choose the former. One has to deal with grief when considering adoption from the good people-bad situation perspective, whereas self-esteem takes the hit in the bad people-good situation perspective. Grief may hurt more, but problems with self-esteem last longer.

Romance. Monica Hill occasionally brings patients to the hospital from a boarding home in Farmington, a country town sixty miles south of St. Louis. One summer evening two years ago while I was working in the emergency room, Monica, wearing a pretty summer outfit, brought in a patient for evaluation. I attended to the patient, finished our business, and bade Monica goodbye. Watching her leave, I wanted to be in her van and her life, heading back to Farmington, which certainly should have had its name changed to Paradise. It always bothered me when Monica came to the hospital because I needed hours to get over her leaving. Monica affected me that way, but so did the daughters of some of my patients, an assistant in prosthetics, a teller at the bank, a nurse in out-patient, the assistant at my dentist's office, and so on and so on. I have always had my nose pressed to the window of the world of some lovely woman who I felt could make my life complete—always, unless running a temperature above 102 degrees.

But these idealizations are wearing thin. While recently covering the emergency room, Monica returned with another patient. I barely noticed her, even though she has hardly changed. She remains attractive, but I did not long to be in her life and remained unmoved when she left. Monica is becoming just another pretty woman and Farmington just another country town, with neither assuming any special importance to me. This probably represents progress; the hospital does not pay me to sit in the emergency room and covet the ladies.

Over the past several years, women are gradually becoming just women, no longer being idealized birthmother substitutes. At an Adoption Congress meeting, for example, many attractive participants attended, but I fell in love with none of them. I simply gave my presentations. In the past, pretty women usually had a depressing effect on me. They made my life and whatever I was doing seem insignificant in contrast to what I imagined life would be like in their world. It wouldn't have helped my presentations if I had believed my efforts to be a waste of time.

Actually, at the conference such a moment occurred. As I sat on a panel, a striking woman clad in a miniskirt entered the room and sat directly in front of our table. For a moment I was unsure whether any words would come out of my mouth when my turn came to speak. My mind became entirely occupied with this woman, and the harder I tried to put her out of my mind, the more she stayed in it. Apparently in situations like this, one does well to confront the distraction directly, but it hardly seemed appropriate to ask this woman to turn her chair around or to have someone stand in front of her. But a minute later I forgot her. In the past, her image would have crowded out everything else in my mind, leaving me functionally decerebrate. It is hard to give a presentation, pitch a game, or carry on any such activity with no useful brain function above the level of the hypothalamus.

I now have an increased capacity to function, but at the price of infrequently falling "in love." As a result of partially grieving the loss of my birthmother, women are becoming just people to me, shaped differently than men to be sure, but no longer goddesses reincarnated from my biological past.

I recently had an interesting conversation about adoption and romance with Joe Soll, an adoptee from New York. We agreed it was an important subject, but also a subject about which little is known. Do male adoptees have more trouble in their romantic lives than female adoptees? (My birthmother friends think so.) Do adoptees pick partners based on their adoptive parents, their birthparents, or neither? Does search and reunion affect choice of romantic partners? Does biology play a role? Joe and I tried to describe to each other the kind of woman that attracts us. Being at a cocktail party, we could point to various people, but even with this added facility I had difficulty expressing myself. Part of the difficulty occurred because my interests have changed. I can no longer project into a birth-mother prototype the expectation that the two of us will magically connect. I know better. This realization changes the game. The woman who interests me today is kinder and gentler than my choice of several years ago. I used to look for someone who could fill the missing part of my life. Now I look for some-one who might help me accept the missing part. Still, change comes haltingly.

Another reason for my relative lack of clarity with Joe was that he probably me caught off guard, for I rarely find someone with whom I can carry on such a conversation. In addition, this area is highly personal and so frequently operative that I, like everyone else, tend to keep it private—all the more reason it should be thoroughly explored. Someday I hope to continue my conversation with Joe.

Authenticity. Hard to describe and difficult to measure, authenticity means different things to different people and nothing at all to some. While one can easily get lost in such terms (i.e., identity, authenticity, integrity, etc.), they are necessary and valid ways to describe people for those of us who hope to be more than behaviorists. Webster defines authentic as "not imaginary, false, or imitation." We should be able to apply this term usefully to adoption issues.

With respect to behavior, authenticity refers to the consistency and relevance of the behavior to the total life of the individual. Authentic actions resonate with the rest of a person's life. They make sense. They result in the lowest level of "entropy." Authentic actions are natural. They endure. For example, I authentically get involved in athletics: I have done so all my life; I have some biological aptitude for it; it comes naturally. Nothing seems imaginary, false, or imitation about my involvement in athletics.

I used to anticipate fitting in with typical middle-class America, although given my history one could hardly imagine how a life-style authentic with that history would fit in with anything typical. Ten years ago I bought a house in suburban St. Louis—America at its best. With two-car garages, brick veneer facades, vaulted ceilings, and bluegrass lawns, I viewed this subdivision as my natural habitat.

I moved in with three large dogs and some fish. Three German Shepherds do not violate the rules of suburbia, but they probably reflect a lifestyle that is not quite mainstream. Over the next several years, my children and I became interested in rabbits. Being frequent visitors to state and county fairs, we became familiar with rabbit shows and often ended up taking home some less distinguished entrants, rabbits that otherwise would have ended up on someone's dinner table.

Our rabbitry prospered. We did little breeding of these rabbits, so almost all of them were "adoptees." I enjoyed taking care of the rabbits and they became important to me. For at least two reasons, I believe the rabbits were associated with my interest in adoption. First, it was hard for me not to identify

No hasenpfeffer here.

with these rabbits, since both they and I had been unwanted. (By the way, rabbits that lose in rabbit shows look pretty much like rabbits that win—I could never tell the difference.) Second, the rabbits provided me with a sense of family when little else did: I had broken ranks with the Andersens, could not locate my natural family, and saw my children only as dictated by a divorce decree. The rabbits, however, were always there; they needed a home and I gave them one. The rabbits, my dogs, and I constituted a family. In the early years of my search, I seriously questioned my activities. It occurred to me that if I became unsuitable to belong to the human community, I could derive purpose in my life by caring for my animals.

Two years later we sheltered forty rabbits in our garage. We did not violate any laws or regulations, they did not constitute a public nuisance, and none of my neighbors complained. (I am eccentric, not stupid.) Still, obviously either the rabbits or I would eventually have to go; one simply does not have forty rabbits in suburbia, legal or not. Logistically, I probably could have continued to manage forty rabbits in my garage without public censure, but this was not certain. Mentally, I developed a conflict between following my heart (keeping the rabbits) versus following my head (keeping the house). I chose to make a decision before being asked to do so: I kept the rabbits and moved to the country. While this would not be the typical decision for most people, it worked for me. Adoptees are often forced to choose between normal and authentic. They do better choosing authentic.

Residents of my backyard.

I have evolved to the belief that society views adoptees as second-class citizens. This conviction has not led me to attempt to change society's view. Instead, I do as little as possible on society's behalf. This strategy avoids wasted effort and makes me feel less abused. My animals have never viewed me as second best. Understandably, therefore I continue to incorporate animals into my life. Ducks swim on my pond, llamas roam my back field, dogs lie around my house; and I enjoy this arrangement. Still, when the sun sets, and three pet turkeys roost on my back porch, I have to wonder if anyone would want to live with someone who has become so eccentric.

Identity. Identity is another abstract term, similar to authenticity. Whereas authenticity relates to what we do, identity refers to what we are. Webster defines identity as "the distinguishing character or personality of an individual."

For most individuals, a major determinant of who they are is their family of origin. Svendsens are different from Kishimotos. Hatfields differ from McCoys. A member of the Kennedys from Massachusetts remains first and foremost a Kennedy, despite whatever else he (or she) does with his (or her) life. Biology plays a major role in defining identities. For me this presented a problem. Pretending I was an Andersen did not make me an Andersen, and this pretense left a void in the part of my identity reserved for biology. I once tried to fill that void with simulations, but biology is not interchangeable. I shared few interests with the Andersens and could not readily graft into their activities. Also, I can not create something out of nothing. Try as I might, I will never be a musician, politician, or actor—these abilities probably do not run in my blood. I do not know what actually runs in my blood, but now know that something does. Cognitively this presented nothing new, but emotionally it did. It is a measure of some emotional growth for me to realize that I, too, have a heritage—albeit one that remains unknown. Through searching I have put a retainer in the part of my identity that once contained a void. Such a retainer does not indicate what belongs there, but it keeps me from putting in things that do not. Also, it places me on the same playing field as everyone else.

The important issue is not that adoptees necessarily learn the specifics of their heritage, but that they come to appreciate they in fact have a heritage. The latter entails more than merely possessing information. All adoptees cognitively know that other human beings gave them birth. Still, one often hears an adoptee involved in searching say that for the first time in his life he realizes he did not hatch from an egg or fall from the sky. This split between emotional and intellectual awareness occurs because feelings toward the birthparents have been repressed. The adoptee must lift this repression, through confrontation of adoption issues, before he can establish his genuine heritage and thereby develop a valid identity. One can only build such an identity on the truth. This truth might be that one's heritage remains unknown, but that in itself is something. Pretense, however, remains merely pretense.

This issue entails more than academic interest. As a cognitive correlate of assuming an identity dissociated from biology, one feels less substantial than others. The consolation phrase "others were expected, I was selected" concomitantly implies that nonadoptees have roots while adoptees do not. A lack of generational continuity adds a degree of vulnerability to all the adoptee's interpersonal relationships. In fact, some experts believe this discontinuity constitutes the core of adoptees' psychological problems.

Not having a sense of biological roots makes it all too easy to overestimate one's adaptive capacity. Frequently, the adoptee is viewed as coming from nowhere and fitting in anywhere. Without roots and raised in an adoptive system that emphasizes nurture over nature, people view the adoptee as a *tabula rasa*, free to become whatever he or she desires—and responsible for it as well. With an excessive sense of adaptability, not carrying on a family tradition, and following in no one's footsteps, the adoptee resembles a pioneer. From this position it becomes easy to try too hard—or to give up altogether.

Some will say I am exaggerating the identity issue. They will argue that adoptees can identify with their adoptive family, follow in adoptive family footsteps, and carry on adoptive family traditions. Perhaps they can, but doing so is often easier said than done; biology does not always cooperate. For example, my adoptive father and I had nothing in common. I liked sports, while he enjoyed home repairs and amateur radio. The distance between these interests precluded significant identifications. Also, if one predicates an identification with the adoptive parents on disavowing one's natural parents, the resulting identification will lack substance and durability. The adoptee shares an identity with two families and cannot substitute one for the other. And two identities are, of course, harder to manage than one.

Lack of Pretense. This issue, less abstract than the previous two, appears relatively clear as it applied to my life: For the first twelve years, the Andersens pretended to be my parents; for the next thirty years, the Andersens and I pretended they were my only parents.

Some will say the Andersens were my real parents because they did the parenting. I disagree. Aunts, uncles, and grandparents raise millions of children every year and the children do not refer to these relatives as mothers and fathers. Parenting and parenthood are not synonymous.

The Andersens raised me. They had the greatest influence on my development. I loved them, or not, in accordance with the quality of our relationship. Aunts, uncles, or grandparents raising a child do not complain about such an arrangement. In these situations people do not push the relationship past its limits. (The children in the television show *Guns of Paradise*, for example, never called Uncle Ethan "Dad.") Adoptive parents often demand more. Perhaps frustrated by their inability to procreate, they overcompensate by claiming exclusive parental dominion over their adoptive children. They frequently insist on being seen as the real parents, the true parents, or the only parents. They are none of these; neither are the birthparents. It makes no more sense to talk about the real, true, or only parents in these circumstances than it does to talk about the real, true, or only child in situations where there is more than one child.

I used to pretend to be an Andersen and pretended in other relationships as well. I do less of that today. But I have fewer relationships.

Assessment. Knowing myself better helps me anticipate my reactions. I no longer feel void of a heritage. I now play basketball, for example, knowing my parents probably pursued athletic interests.   Such a realization relaxes me because it suggests I am just following tradition, not blazing new trails. Feeling part of a group, I do not press as hard as I once did. While I do not know my actual heritage, I know it determines my options. Adoptees are not as adaptable as people expect. I no longer try to be.

Guilt. My adoptive mother would have been horrified had I asked her about my birthmother, and I would have assumed the responsibility for her distress. Actually, my father reacted with anger more than hurt to my search, and disagreements over my adoption eventually terminated our relationship. Stanley's death did not sadden me. If anything, I felt relieved that his $35,000-a-year nursing home bill finally ended. I regretted that my search upset my father, but saw that as his problem, not mine. Searching usually strengthens adoptive relationships. It made mine worse. The rule probably reads: Searching strengthens good relationships and weakens bad ones.

Self-awareness and Increased Comfort. In the past I decided how to feel (largely trying to meet parental expectations) and attempted to force my emotions to comply. Now I begin with my emotions and work back the other way. I assume that my reactions are rooted in my heritage and life history and are thereby worthy of consideration.

Other. I used to work half time in private practice and half time for the Veteran's Administration. In part as a result of having dealt with my adoption, I left private practice and joined the VA full time, reflecting my shifting identification in the direction of less privileged individuals. I became a vegetarian, not for religious or health reasons, but because I like animals too much to eat them. And I own gold stocks because I am not bullish on

America—which probably reflects my feeling that society fumbled the ball on my adoption.

I am happy with my changes (minus the gold stocks). These changes occurred only after I dealt with my adoption; they probably occurred because I dealt with my adoption.

Chapter Twelve

Whys and wherefores

> A man who has been the indisputable favorite of his
> mother keeps for life the feeling of a conqueror, that
> confidence of success that often induces real success.
> —*Sigmund Freud*

Adoptees develop more emotional problems than nonadoptees. That should not surprise anyone. Adoptees constitute perhaps twenty percent of the adolescents known to mental health professionals, which represents a ten-fold increase above the expected rate. Adoptees present themselves with behavior disorders, adjustment reactions, substance abuse, and depression. They are not at higher risk for schizophrenia, phobias, sexual disorders, or manic-depressive disease. Adult adoptees are not as overrepresented in the clinical population as are adolescents.

Parents do not treat adoptees grossly different than non-adoptees. No one locks them in cages at night, deprives them of medical care, or feeds them table scraps. They receive presents on their birthdays and do not end up two inches shorter than nonadoptees. Adoptees confront abstract and diffuse conflicts. Consistent with these conflicts, they develop abstract and diffuse problems. Adoptees tend to have low self-esteem, lack self-confidence, feel incomplete, and lack a sense of belonging. These are difficult issues to identify and resolve. Compliant adoptees live with these problems, often becoming depressed. Rebellious adoptees externalize their problems, often getting into conflict with society.

Certain things about adoption are unavoidably traumatic —even perfect adoptive parents cannot obviate these problems. No good way exists to sugarcoat maternal rejection, and everyone views adoption as a second-choice way to form a family. However, adoptees raised by empathic, loving parents do better than those who are not.

Adoption per se is not really the problem; more accurately, unwanted children present the problem. Adoption provides perhaps the best way to deal with families that can not or will not raise their own children. But adoption becomes a problem itself when people encourage it as the option of choice, without first making every effort to keep the children with their natural families. As part of the business of baby brokering, adoption becomes child abuse. Adoptive parents should realize that they make it difficult to resolve adoptive conflicts if they begin their family by exploiting their child's birthparents.

Efforts to explain adoptee problems range from biological to philosophical, from ridiculous (unconscious comparisons to bowel movements) to sublime (genealogical bewilderment). It has been suggested that out-of-wedlock pregnancy can be an indicator of psychiatric illness. Some think unmarried mothers fail to obtain prenatal care, thereby predisposing their children to minimal brain damage. Adoptive parents have been viewed as causing problems by being overprotective (out of fear of losing their children), oversolicitous (as a result of having to prove themselves superior parents), or averse to parenthood (expressed as an inability to conceive). The adoptee has been seen as narcissistically injured as a result of his mother's rejection, unable to resolve family romance fantasies because he has two sets of parents, prone to split parents into bad adoptive-good biological or vice versa, unable to negotiate oedipal conflicts because of a weakened incest taboo, and disposed to act out negative fantasies as a result of identifications with denigrated birthparents.

Since these explanations tend to be abstract and theoretical, they fail to inspire conviction. Genealogical bewilderment was recently offered as a reason why the California State Legislature should unseal adoption records. It didn't help. Genealogical bewilderment is a lovely term—poetic, provocative, and profound—but you can't take it to the bank (or to state legislatures). No one understands what it means.

I wish to talk about the problems I faced as an adoptee. I will try to draw as much as possible from my actual experience, but some issues will necessarily remain conjectural because factors outside my awareness influenced me. While my situation was unusual, it should be possible to generalize from my experience. I was sold rather than placed, adopted at fourteen years rather than fourteen weeks, but I was raised by and given the name of people to whom I was not biologically connected—and that is the bottom line in extrafamilial adoptions.

Loss of Innocence. Larry Inman and I ran around together during high school and college. After graduation, Larry went to Vietnam. I went to St. Louis. My world remained a matter of touch-football games, exam scores, and Saturday night parties. His became one of PT boats, body counts, and quad-50 machine guns. Upon his return, Larry no longer viewed society as he had prior to Vietnam. Life had lost the innocence it possessed when it consisted merely of playing high school football or studying college chemistry; shooting people has a way of doing that. To a greater or lesser degree, so does learning you were given away. Abandonment, like war, is serious business. My world changed forever upon learning of my adoption. It became a less friendly, more sober, less comfortable place to live.

All adoptees must deal with the fact their mothers did not keep them. That realization does not foster self-confidence. Lost forever is the sense of invulnerability that goes with having been wanted and special in the eyes of the most important person in one's life.   It is impossible not to feel responsible for the abandonment. People speak of motherhood in the same breath as God, country, and apple pie. One faces a major problem of cognitive dissonance trying to reconcile the venerable concept of mother with the fact that she gave you away. Tradition favors mother and makes the odds seem pretty good that the problem resided with you. Over time one develops an increased capacity to understand and accept this experience, but the earlier position is never entirely abandoned.

Only recently, for example, I met an attractive, vivacious, Harvard graduate adoptee and puzzled over why her mother gave *her* away. Conversely, several months ago upon meeting an adoptee with a cleft palate, I instinctively "realized" why his mother left *him*. Certainly these assumptions are incorrect. I understand why birthmothers give up their children. Still, somewhere in my mind I obviously see the adoptee as responsible for the abandonment—and I try very hard to be rational about these things.

Birthmothers regularly proclaim they were forced into relinquishing their children. Their position is understandable; if I had been one of them, I probably would have done the same thing. Yet as an adoptee, their statements fail to move me. My feelings transcend logic. When I think of my birthmother, part of me will always idealize her. Somewhere in my mind, my mother is beautiful, loving, and good—because I want her to be.

And part of me will always be hurt because this "wonderful" person walked out of my life.

Even at a logical level the rejection issue persists. A fourteen-year-old girl may not be able to support and raise a child, but her extended family almost always can. The birth-mother may be pushed into her decision, but her family generally does the pushing; and they do so by choice. I take no comfort in having been rejected by my whole clan, rather than just by my mother.

Personality Basics. Ann Andersen did not have the same kind of experience caring for me as would a mother with her natural child. For one thing, biological factors play a role in early mother-child relationships. In addition, I failed to affirm Ann Andersen of her femininity, sexuality, or generativity—quite the contrary, I reminded her of her limitations. She faced other problems as well and had not emotionally adjusted to the many changes of her life. Also, Ann worried that I might be taken away. Because of these things, her enthusiasm for our early relationship probably remained limited.

The Andersens thought poorly of my birthparents. Giving away your kin is bad enough, but in my day it equated with promiscuity, which prior to penicillin was viewed more severely than in later years. The Andersens did not talk about my birthparents, but they never forgot them and undoubtedly manifested their feelings nonverbally.

One cannot easily maintain secrets and keep a close relationship. Imagine how much fun a husband would have with his wife at an office party if he is carrying on an affair with his secretary. The Andersens always had to watch what they said around me. Keeping secrets set us apart. Buying me through the black market caused them to worry about losing me. Developing closeness under these conditions was difficult.

Early interpersonal relationships affect personality. One can more easily be outgoing and confident if he was greeted in his initial years with enthusiasm and affirmation rather than ambivalence and doubt. My relationship with the Andersens determined part of my personality. I do not instinctively expect the doors of life to open wide, allowing me to be eagerly greeted in a warm embrace. For some people the doors never close. These people probably had attentive, empathic, emotionally invested parents. I envy them. I admire them. I am not one of them.

That is all right; not everyone is warm, fuzzy, and outgoing. The world accommodates plenty of roles, and they all do not require a person to be a great after-dinner speaker or have an infectious smile. My problem entailed not so much who I was, but how I felt about who I was. I used castigate myself for not being a hail-fellow-well-met kind of person. I would have done better to appreciate my assets.

Pam, a birthmother in my CUB (Concerned United Birthparents) group, thinks she can identify adoptees by their lack of self-esteem. Perhaps she can. She has become upset with the daughter she placed for adoption because this daughter lacks self-confidence. The adopted daughter contrasts with her five other children (all raised with her), whom she describes as confident, outgoing, and secure. Pam derides her adopted daughter about her insecurity, viewing it as a character flaw (although she also blames the birthfather). Pam does not seem to consider that this daughter's insecurity might stem from her adoption. Adoption is not a stroll in the park. It is a major stress. As such, it often determines basic components of the adoptee's personality. We would do better to appreciate this fact. It does not help Pam's daughter that her birthmother chides her about her insecurity. It did not help me that I wanted to be someone else.

Lying. Lying, never a pretty topic, constituted an important part of my relationship with the Andersens. Until I turned twelve, the Andersens implicitly lied about being my parents. They then told me my birthparents died in an automobile accident (a lie).

They fabricated that I was born at St. Luke's Hospital in Chicago, at 5:15 A.M. on April 16th, and that I weighed 8 pounds, 7 ounces—all untrue. They lied to the church, to the state, to their families, and to me. The lies began when they took me home and ended when they died. If nothing else, they remained consistent. I came to hate the lies. That the Andersens so systematically and inclusively distorted the truth says something about their sense of authority over me. At best, it indicates they felt justified in being dishonest. At worst, it implies a sense of ownership. At any level, I resent it.

People lose credibility when they lie. This presents no problem if the liar is a used-car salesman, but it becomes important when one's mother and father do the lying. We learn our basic sense of trust from our parents. When they are not trustworthy, the whole world becomes suspect. Also, we don't like people who lie to us—even our parents.

Lies abound in adoption. There are outright lies ("Your parents were killed in an auto accident"), and white lies (the chosen child story, "Your mother loved you so much she gave you up"). People tell outright lies solely to benefit themselves. They tell white lies for more noble reasons, but white lies probably end up doing more harm than good. White lies are told to prevent the adoptee from being hurt and often involve attempting to deny differences between adopted and natural—for example, my father's statement that he always treated me as if I were his real son. (This particular lie tripped all over itself from its inception; lies have a way of doing that.) Comments by adoptive parents that they view their child as a real (natural) child merely reduce their credibility. Society does not view adoptive children as natural children—they view them as adoptive children. So do adoptive parents. That's just the way it is.

Even well-intended lying presents problems because it presumes an unequal relationship. The (well-intended) liar essentially says, "I know what is best for you and determine that you are better off ignorant rather than upset." Even if this judgment is correct, the person being lied to will take offense. The major psychological insult to adoptees is their lack of self-determination, and lying continues to undermine this capacity.

Being Alone.   During Germany's bombing of England, the English thought they could protect their children by moving them away from the cities to the relative safety of the countryside. To their surprise, they found that children who remained with their parents, even under attack, did better than those who were moved. Being separated from their parents proved more traumatic to the children than the bombing.

Adoptees resemble the children moved to the countryside. Whatever stigma goes with their abandonment, they face alone. If medical problems run in their family, no one in their personal world carries the same risks. If their past has criminal behavior, alcoholism, immorality, or insanity, these issues cannot be fully shared by adoptive relatives. It is probably less stressful psychologically to deal with real problems as a member of a family of rapists and pillagers than to deal with imaginary problems alone.

Several years ago a St. Louis judge stated at an adoption conference that she favored open records—unless she found something so awful that it was better left alone. What a pleasant inference. What is so awful it must be left alone? Chain saw massacres are not left alone—people make movies about them. Is it worse than that? What did the judge expect an adoptee would do upon hearing the horrible truth? Kill himself? Kill someone else? Burn the flag? Are adoptees really so vulnerable that the truth will push them over the edge? If so, maybe we should have our telephones removed and our mail screened so someone doesn't give us this information and thereby transform us into vengeful kamikazes.

One faces the dark side of adoption alone. My adoption appeared so "dangerous" that it did not surface even through twelve years of psychoanalysis. Adoptees worry about why they were given away, and no one believes it was due to a consummate act of love. Thinking about one's adoption defines limits (as does opening records). Fantasies become less frightening when put into words. Leave the fantasies preverbal, stir them up, think about them by yourself in the middle of the night, and they become terrifying—they have a way of ruining the following day. One doesn't want to get down and boogie on Saturday night when Saturday morning begins with a nightmare.

If something is so awful the family can't discuss it and judges must conceal it, how does one know the adoptive family can withstand its revelation? Relationships then depend on this "awful" fact remaining secret. If adoptees are chosen, they can be rejected. My father was ready to disown me because of my search. What would he have done if he had learned I was the product of incest? The adoptive brother of a woman in our ALMA group committed murder. Neighbors consoled his adoptive father with the statement that the boy wasn't "really" his son. I wouldn't be proud if my son murdered someone, but I couldn't extricate myself from the situation by impugning heredity. An adoptee in the movie *Lace* is consoled by his adoptive mother, who had seduced him into years of incest, by her explanation that she wasn't really his mother. Well, are we "real" children or not? The answer seems to be determined by convenience.

One of my German Shepherds is not by nature courageous. When I take only her for a walk, I must carry her past an area where neighbor dogs bark at her through their fence. However, when another dog goes with her, she boldly barks and tugs like a guard dog. She has more confidence as a part of a group. So do people. For the adoptee, that group membership is conditional. There always remains a question whether the adoptive family will revoke their choice. As such, the adoptee does not share the primitive security that comes with tribal blood membership. At a basic level, this lack of security affects how securely one moves through the world.

Finally, one should note that the Islamic world does not practice adoption. Children may be raised by other families, but they keep their natural names—not a bad idea. In Islamic culture one's responsibility for blood relatives preempts all other responsibilities. This responsibility even extends to being expected to exact revenge for those relatives who cannot do so themselves (scary?). People without blood ties stand alone (or perhaps form support groups). Can we assume that five hundred million people have nothing to teach us about human nature?

Idealization.   I have had difficulty bringing my birthmother down to earth. I have loved her and hated her, but she has always lived above the clouds. Everyone's mother initially resides with the gods, but she usually comes down to earth when the weather clears. Repression has a way of keeping the weather inclement. Also, one more reluctantly leaves a goddess if he has never lived with her.

The birthmothers in my CUB group remain intensely invested in the children they relinquished. Neither time, subsequent children, nor efforts to forget have attenuated their wish to mother their lost children. Often during search and reunion the birthmother's emotional investment in the adopted child preempts all other relationships. I see the emotional investment a natural mother has in her child. I am envious of this kind of attachment. I have not experienced being special to anyone in that way. I never will be. Ann Andersen was, in part, just going through the motions. My birthmother chose to leave. Subsequent relationships are less magical than that of early mother and child. I continue to look for the magic.

We search more for our image of the person we have lost than for the actual person. It surprises adoptees to find parents who are no longer young, as it surprises birthparents to find children who have grown up. Unconsciously we expect reunions to be timeless. My fantasies of blissful reunion do not envision me as a fifty-year-old man and my birthmother a seventy-year-old woman. I picture us a bit more youthful. One can do that in fantasies.

Not long ago I met with several adoptees in Milwaukee. We stayed at one of their homes, which happens to be about two miles from where I may have been born. Although not completely crazy, I had the fantasy that when Dori opened her door I would be met, as a special surprise, by my birthmother. Having just seen *Pretty Woman* several days before my trip, I had fallen in love with Miss Vivian. The mother I expected to meet upon entering the house was not a sixty-eight-year-old, retired dental technician from West Allis, but Miss Vivian from Hollywood. Incidents like that probably happen often in my mind, although rarely are they as obvious. In our idealized world of reunions, all the men are strong; all the women are beautiful; and all the children, well above average. It is hard to leave the fairy tale.

Guilt. The Andersens brought me into their family to relieve Ann Andersen's depression. More succinctly, they acquired me to help prevent her suicide. Once there, like the Dutch boy with his finger in the dike, it proved difficult to leave. This issue became one of my most difficult conflicts, pitting Ann Andersen's emotional stability against my need for authenticity. The Andersens expected me to be the child they could not conceive. To avoid hurting my adoptive mother (perhaps fatally), I tried to comply. Their needs and mine clashed on this issue.

The Andersens pretended I was their child, thereby denying the pain associated with their infertility. Once they used me in this way, they expected me to remain a permanent prop in their psychological defenses. The situation made my natural impulses dangerous because those impulses undermined the Andersens' emotional stability. My authentic actions hurt the Andersens and I felt responsible for their pain. That was why it took me only several seconds to "forget" my birthfamily upon learning of my position in the Andersen family. That was why my adoption did not come up throughout twelve years of psychoanalysis. This conflict encompassed far more than whether I thought about my birthmother on Mother's Day. It dealt with whether my instincts were dangerous, and it played out in areas far removed from adoption.

For example, I sometimes jog around the VA hospital. My course necessarily takes me by the spinal cord unit, where in the summertime patients often sit outside in wheelchairs. I used to feel guilty running by these patients and worried that my running would depress them by reminding them of what they could no longer do. I feared that one might try to harm himself. I worried the administration would bring action against me for gross insensitivity. I worried that I might really be insensitive. While adoption is not overtly involved in this example, the dynamics duplicate those with my adoptive parents.

Striking out a lot of batters in a softball game, I worried that I might humiliate an opposing player. If one of these players was going through a bad phase in his life, my behavior might push him over the edge. At worst, he might kill himself; at best, I would prove myself to be a selfish jerk. Again, the dynamics relate to my adoption. My mother's potential suicide or the imminent revelation of my callous insensitivity has shadowed my every authentic move. Calamity has never been more than one spontaneous step away: Pitching softball was going to ruin my medical career; our dogs might give us hookworms; the rabbits could transmit tularemia; buying gold stocks would bring my financial ruin; becoming vegetarian might produce a nutritional deficiency; our country home would be infested with copperheads; jogging by the spinal cord unit would cost me my job; moving offices would ruin my medical practice; my comment to Aunt Shirley could kill my mother. These concerns appear foolish now. They did not seem foolish at the time.

I cannot fully convey the adverse effects of this conflict—putting it into words limits the scope. I worried about hurting others, hurting myself, and being an insensitive person. It has taken me a lifetime to appreciate that if my actions hurt someone it is not necessarily my fault, my problem, or my responsibility. No one deserves credit that the Andersens held me responsible for their emotional stability. That aspect of my adoption should never have happened.

Utility: Three llamas roam my back field. Their job is to be llamas. We don't eat them, shear them, or make them pull little carts at children's parties. I enjoy watching them do llama things, and it pleases me that they enjoy their lives. I try to provide for my animals an environment philosophically different from the one provided for me. The Andersens did not bring me into their family simply to enjoy having me around and derive pleasure from watching me develop. Stanley and Ann Andersen purchased me in large part to resolve their emotional problems. My situation was not unusual in this respect. In general, adoptees assume a more utilitarian function in their families than do natural children. Natural children, being physical and emotional extensions of their parents, more readily provide narcissistic identifications for their parents. Adoptees, being at best only emotional extensions of their parents, are less likely to provide such identifications. Typically, adoptive parents ask what the adoptee can do for them, before they ask what they can do for the adoptee.

My conflicts were (are) not unique; most adoptees must deal with similar issues, although perhaps to a different degree. The Andersens kept more secrets than most adoptive parents, they lied more than most, and they worried more that I might be taken away. Otherwise, my adoptive experience was not unusual. My adoption issues were exacerbated by their mismanagement; but, on the other hand, I was placed at three days and thus spared the problems of being in temporary or foster care. Also, the Andersens subjected me to no gratuitous abuse. Perhaps my conflicts more directly involved adoption issues than did the conflicts of some other adoptees. I fared better than many. There are some real horror stories out there. I don't consider mine one of them.

A matter of philosophy.

Chapter Thirteen
Retrospect

Most of our future lies ahead.
—*Denny Crum*

My daughter asked if this book would end pro or con adoption. Her question seemed off base. Adoption, like amputation, is not something one stands for or against; it is something that at times has to be done and hopefully can be handled as humanely as possible. Recently, however, people have raised questions about adoption itself. Many birthparents find adoption immoral and consider even orphanages as preferable. I doubt they will garner much support for the orphanage idea, but other options exist. Reuben Pannor, for example, prefers permanent guardianship to adoption. Certainly guardianship would help solve the problem of adoptive parents pretending their children are natural. In my day permanent guardianship would not have been a viable option because babies flooded the market. Permanent guardianship makes more sense today, although open adoption might be preferable—if it can be made to work.

Bob Ralls, my best friend from high school, called recently to give his reaction to my manuscript. Bob wanted to be
honest. He stated that in his opinion the Andersens were simply
inadequate parents. He remembers my house was always dark
and that my parents never made him feel welcome. He found
them to be cold, critical people (of both him and me) and
thought my problems might be due more to their personalities
than to the adoption.

I have always admired Bob. When he speaks, I listen.
But on this issue, while we share similar observations, we arrive
at different conclusions. The two of us agree my home carried
a depressive tone, which probably came from my mother. And
we agree that my parents were not warm, outgoing people, although this might have been due more to their insecurity and
perhaps their cultural style than to condescension. Certainly I
never heard them criticize Bob, nor were they especially critical
of me, except about my emotional responsiveness. They probably did not make Bob feel welcome, perhaps out of jealousy.
Bob and I related well. My parents and I did not. Also, when
Bob and I got together, we typically played catch, shot baskets,
or visited friends. Therefore I usually left the house, and my
parents may have resented my absence. The Andersens might
have been cool to Bob because they did not welcome his presence, although through no fault of his.

Bob, now the director of a youth agency, believes that the
success of an adoption depends largely on the personalities of
the adoptive parents. In part, I agree. Obviously, loving adoptive parents, who have worked through their losses, respect their
child's heritage, and empathize with and tolerate their child's
losses are better than cold, insensitive parents. Unfortunately,
few couples achieve such competence; most have to struggle
with adoption issues. Also, while the adoption is influenced by
the personalities of the adoptive parents, the personalities of the
adoptive parents are influenced by the adoption. For example,
Ann Andersen might have avoided depression had she not

developed cancer at age twenty-two. The Andersens perhaps could have become more congenial if they had not been concealing so many secrets. My father might have been more relaxed around a couple of kids who shared his abilities, rather than a couple of jocks who intimidated him. Personalities are not closed systems. Situations affect personalities, personalities affect situations. I understand what Bob says about my adoptive parents, but their personalities do not eliminate the adoption as an issue. In my opinion, my adoptive parents were good-enough people who miserably bungled the adoption and then had to live with the consequences.

My history provides a gold mine (a bad metaphor considering what I have learned about gold mines) of information on how not to handle an adoption. My parents could not have managed the adoption issue worse.   Lessons can be learned from our experience.

For adoptive parents:

1. Do not buy a baby through the black market. After buying a baby it becomes awkward to attempt to adopt him. Stanley and Ann Andersen constantly worried about losing me and could not discuss their concerns with anyone for fear of leaking information about my status. A similar situation presents itself in the case of a child obtained in any compromised manner.

2. Do not adopt until you have worked through your losses. Making the adoptee responsible for the adoptive parents' emotional stability presents a cruel and unnecessary burden. No one benefits.

3. Tell the child of his adoption. The earlier, the better. If adoptive parents have worked through their losses, they can be sensitive to their child's interests and gauge their statements to the

level of the child's concern. Much has been written about the best time to tell the child, most of it drivel. The child must integrate two sets of parents, and the sooner, the better. If the matter bothers him too much, he will leave it alone. The critical issue for the adoptive parents is to have worked through their insecurities, so they can be sensitive to the child's concerns and need not ignore the adoption—or compulsively beat the child over the head with it.

4. Don't lie. It costs too much, even if the lie is never overtly confirmed.

5. Expect your child to search. (He may not.) Parents can have more than one child. Children can have more than two parents. Throwing yourself across the path of search can result in serious injury.

For adoptees:

1. One can be unaware of the importance of his adoption. It took me thirty years to confront my adoption. Ignorance was not bliss. Adoption issues affected my life, whether I acknowledged them or not, and became magnified because they were ignored. Adoption plays a big role in the life of every adoptee. Start with that assumption.

2. Expect to be sad. Adoption entails loss, for all triad members. One resolves loss through grief. No grief, no growth.

3. Remember transference. The unconscious mind remains un-constrained by logic. It is timeless and fluid. Look for your birthmother (father) in the love of your life, rather than the love of your life in your birthmother (father).

4. React. Do something with your adoption. Ask questions, read, reflect, consider, and fashion a response that makes sense to you. "The great affair is to move."

5. Expect to be angry. Conscious anger fuels self-assertion (although unconscious anger often leads to guilt and inhibition). The compliant, inhibited adoptee is someone who cannot accept his or her anger.

For birthparents:

1. You are important to your child, but ambivalently so. The adoptee can more easily forgive (if that is relevant) than forget. You may love your child and your child may love you, but the timing is bad and you will always be, in part, out of synch.

2. Life goes on. Don't ignore the rest of you life trying to turn back the clock with your son or daughter. Trying to relive the past can mess up the present.

For professionals:

1. The adoption will be an important issue. Listen for it. Listen for it directly when the subject is obviously adoption, but also indirectly in other material the adoptee brings in.

2. An issue may be related to adoption even if the adoptee says it is not; consider resistance. But adoption isn't everything. It can also be used defensively to avoid other problems; again, consider resistance.

3. Adoption issues can be resolved (effectively, if not completely), and what might have once been a major conflict may no longer be actively important if the person has sufficiently dealt with it.

Growing up in an adoptive family differs from growing up in a natural family. Raising an adopted child differs from raising a natural child. Adoption is a second-choice way to form a family. Everyone should recognize this fact. But they don't. Children do not dream of growing up and raising someone else's children—they dream of growing up and having their own. Couples adopt children largely for one reason: They cannot have their own. If a couple prefers adoption to having their own children, they are probably unfit as parents. Blood is thicker than water. Societies recognize this fact. But adoptive families do not, perhaps because they feel invalid unless they simulate natural families.

My son attends Northeast Missouri State University. He plays baseball there. Northeast plays in NCAA Division II. The big schools (Missouri, Michigan, Auburn, Florida State) play Division I. Most children who get into athletics grow up hoping to someday play for a Division I school. They end up in Division II when they are not quite good enough to play Division I. This doesn't mean, however, that Division II games are less exciting, that the players get less satisfaction, or that the parents are less interested and proud. Division II is not Division I, but the players, fans, and parents don't care. It is not any less satisfying. Unless the student anticipates a career as a professional athlete, it can be more satisfying.

Adoption parallels playing Division II. It is everybody's second choice. Accepting this fact allows one to appreciate what adoption is, rather than what it is not. Adoption is real. Adoption is not natural. Adoptive children can be loved as much as natural children, and adoptive parents loved as much as natural parents. Adoption falls apart when people expect it to simulate natural. Taken for what it is, adoption is a valid, vital, durable relationship. Differences exist. Recognize the differences. Accept the differences. Perhaps, even celebrate the differences.

On a personal level my situation has little changed. I recently went to Milwaukee and stood inside a room that could have been my birthplace. A sacred quality imbued the room, which I might have better appreciated had the owner not been so chatty. I considered parking permanently outside this house until my mother returned, but discounted the idea as impractical.

Maybe the time has come to resume my search. Previous leads have played out, but it might be worthwhile to start tracing people who have a birth certificate signed by Doctor Trump or Theresa Kusiak. Recently I have been occupied with writing. When I finish this book, I should have more energy to search. It seems a little scary that recording one's history partially creates that history, for things included gain ascendence over those left out. Once a view is established, it becomes entrenched. I trust, however, that I have written as accurately as possible. Writing this book helped clarify my adoption experience and conflicts; more than that, it helped me react to my adoption. Intrinsic satisfactions like these are nice because sometimes that's all there is.

I wrote this book with adoptees in mind. Hopefully, it will interest other triad members as well. If one of you reading this book happens to be a birthmother who in April 1940 was in a Milwaukee residential neighborhood awaiting the birth of your child, perhaps that child was me. If so, I would like to say hello. I wish I could have known you. I think of you often.

The Cover: The front photograph includes the Andersen family and Ann's brother Frank. Technical assistance for implimenting the cover design was provided by John Greaves.

About the Author

Robert Andersen received his medical degree from Washington University in St. Louis and took his psychiatry training at St. Louis University. He is currently Chief of the Mental Health Clinic at the St. Louis Veterans Administration Medical Center and lives in the St. Louis metropolitan area with his son and a variety of animals.

Doctor Andersen has published six articles, on a variety of subjects from prisoners of war to baseball. Two of the articles (in *Child Welfare*) deal with adoption. He also wrote a chapter on the psychology of running in the book *The Complete Runner, Volume II*.

At age three days Robert Andersen was sold through the black market for $250.

Order Form

Badger Hill Press
P.O. Box 4066
Chesterfield, Missouri 63006-4066
Phone/Fax (314) 272-7819

Please send me *Second Choice: growing up adopted.*
ISBN: 0-9632648-4-2   paperback $10.00

Number of copies_____

Name_____

Address_____

City_____State_____

Zip_____

Sales tax: Missouri residents please add 6%

Shipping: Book rate is $2.00 for first book and 75 cents each
additional book. Airmail: $3.50 per book.